This book is dedicated to Sylvie,
and
to Caterina and to Maximilien,

with warm thanks to Jonathan and to Jim
and
with appreciation for the legacy of an elder Max and of Nick and J-J

First Edition 2009

UK Legal Deposit Libraries Act, 2003: British Library Cataloguing in Publication Data; Data applied for

© Musei Vaticani: World-wide rights secured for cover colour photograph of Raphael's "The School of Athens:"
© Express Newspapers: Giles cartoon on p. 133: permission applied for

ISBN   978-2-9533867-0-7   UK English Paperback Edition

Published in 2009 by
        La Rémige SARL,
        11 bis boulevard Delessert,
        75016 Paris,
        France
        www.laremige.com

Also by Robert Gillespie: "Soft Underbelly" a novel - La Rémige Publishers, 2009

Machiavelli and The Mayflower

How to Understand the Europeans

by Bob Gillespie

CONTENTS

INTRODUCTION

AUTHOR'S FOREWORD TO THE FIRST EDITION

CHAPTER 1   POLITICS AND RELIGION   1

CHAPTER 2   ROMANISM   11

CHAPTER 3   MONARCHISM   41

CHAPTER 4   REFORMISM   61

CHAPTER 5   REPUBLICANISM   81

CHAPTER 6   RECOGNISING CARICATURES   99

CHAPTER 7   DEMOGRAPHICS AND THE GRID   119

CHAPTER 8   USING THE GRID TO UNDERSTAND BEHAVIOUR   126

CHAPTER 9   INTERACTIONS AND CONTRASTS   136

GLOSSARY   155

BIBLIOGRAPHY   161

APPENDICES   162

INDEX   177

INTRODUCTION

INTRODUCTION

*The Master said, "In his errors a man is true to type; observe
the errors and you will know the man."*
Confucius, Book IV

The British who live and work in France, that magnificent
country, rich in history and tradition, live nonetheless in a culture
far from their own. Most Brits are happy "across the water,"
because their genes help them to be so: the reputedly national
British phlegm equips them to take cultural frustration in their
stride, and their reputed sense of irony prepares them even to
smile at it.

What do they notice about the locals, who are not necessarily so
phlegmatic nor as ironic as they? For example, have they finally
accepted that their neighbours don't care about being on time?
Are they fed up listening to pious locals stating that poverty is
close to sanctity, or do some of them admit that wealth can be
God-given and that it actually signifies *divine approval*? Do they
believe that owning up is naïve, or that it is the "honourable"
thing to do? Do they keep promises only if it suits them, or do
they believe promises are *made* to be kept? Do they worry more
about rights and duties, or about fairness and pragmatism? Do
they believe themselves responsible, but certainly not guilty, or
do they think they carry the can? Do they believe that the state is
there for them, or do they rather ask themselves what can they do
for *it*?

Our European ancestors are both guilty of, and responsible for,
the religious and political ideals at the root of such beliefs: they
set the scene for the monumental squabbles of the pre-, and post-,
Reformation thinkers; of the Swiss, Jean-Jacques Rousseau,

publishing the merits of his vision of a republic in 'The Social Contract' almost 30 years before the French Revolution; of the sly Niccolò Machiavelli who, long before, educated his 'Prince' on how to avoid one.

Machiavelli was an outrageous thinker, whose abrasive advice, gleaned from the medieval antics of the notorious Italian Borgias, has probably guided as many a recent-day corporate executive, as medieval prince, in the arts of surviving the labyrinths of power. If Louis XVI's head didn't survive the onslaught of the French Republic, is it because he hadn't read his Machiavelli, and so, found himself disastrously overtaken by Rousseau's seditious statements on the quasi sanctity of a republican constitution? Where was Louis's 'Magna Carta' when he needed one?

Because those *phlegmatic* barons wielding the Magna Carta under King John's nose at Runnymede left the royal head sitting on its shoulders, *ironically*, they changed the course of history. How British to have left the king his head! How very 'fair play,' (and Cricket hadn't even been invented in 1215!) The Magna Carta ensured the survival of the most far reaching of British institutions, and this despite Oliver Cromwell's extensive study of it; a hundred years before Jean-Jacques Rousseau, from Switzerland, and Thomas Paine, in America, inflamed their readers with republican, anti monarchical zeal, Britain's burghers took a republic for a test drive, and found it wanting! Why? Because King John's 13th century barons had left an enduring legacy to the British people, a religiously committed and non-politically-elected head of state, otherwise said, the prototype of a *constitutional* monarch and the coup de grace for British feudalism!

The sixty three clauses of the Magna Carta, drawn up at a time when enlightenment was not even a glint in the eye of any eighteenth century thinker, set a foundation for the values embodied in British attitudes to privilege, to money, to honour, to dignity, to personal responsibility, to nationhood. Such attitudes

INTRODUCTION

are a reference against which the British measure their culture gap with others.[1]

A few hundred years later, European Christianity stirred the primal stew that led to the Reformation. Amid the turmoil, Louis XIV saw fit to chase away the protestant Huguenots, and, if we are to believe the early 20th century German sociologist, Max Weber, so give up a final, historic opportunity for France of ever fully understanding capitalism. Is it not ironic that we must thank a son of *France* for the Protestant Work Ethic? If, as Weber claimed, the roots of capitalism spring from Calvinist Protestantism, let us ever thank the French, (who are, at last count, about 82% Roman Catholic,) for the work of Jean Calvin, and his doctrines that identify worldly wealth with divine favour in the teeth of Catholic teaching.

The very Englishness of Nicholas Breackspear from Abbots Langley in Hertfordshire provoked mutiny in the French monasteries, offended a German Emperor, and sowed near panic among the Italian nobility; according to the French historian, Jacques Mercier, the Romans found Nicholas unpredictable, disturbingly *phlegmatic*, and they misunderstood his use of *irony*. Phlegm and irony! That sounds British! Who was Nicholas Breackspear, anyway? He was Adrian IV, Britain's first ever English Pope......and Britain's last! The year was 1156, only 90 years after William Plantagenet's celebrated one way crossing to that big island off the Normandy coast.

Nicholas Breackspear's continental difficulties would show that the reputedly British unpredictable, phlegmatic and ironic

---

[1] WHEREFORE WE WISH AND FIRMLY ENJOIN that the English Church shall be free, and that men in our kingdom shall have and keep all these liberties, rights, and concessions, well and peaceably in their fullness and entirety for themselves and their heirs, of us and of our heirs, in all things and all places for ever.
Both we and the barons have sworn that all this shall be observed in good faith and without deceit. Witness the above-mentioned people and many others.
Given by our hand in the meadow that is called Runnymede, between Windsor and Staines, on the fifteenth day of June in the seventeenth year of our reign
Magna Carta #63

personality was already formed and flourishing at the turn of the first millennium, and this would appear as evidence that at least these cultural traits were already firmly ensconced in Hastings *before* the Norman cavalry arrived, and *not* after. Nicholas returned to his maker long before the European bewilderment of the early 16th century, but would his phlegmatic and ironic English Holiness really have balked at the linearity, the pragmatism, the sense of personal responsibility, the regard for frugality and for worldly virtue, and the sense of national pride that the Reformation is reputed to have fostered? I think not, because he was, after all, a "Brit." If Britain's only English pope ever was already struggling in 1156 to get the Romans to laugh at his jokes, then, we are talking here about an isotope of 'Britishness' that has a very long half life indeed.

The historical point of departure of the Reformation is held to be when Martin Luther nailed his 95 theses to the door of Wittenberg Castle Church in 1517. The Vatican agonized for almost three decades in misadventure and indecision over how to react, not only to the German princes supporting the Protestant movement, but also to the amorous foibles of Henry VIII. In 1542, Pope Paul III convened the Council of Trent with themes on Revelation; Original Sin and Justification, and the Nature of the Sacraments, all to treat the scepticism of the new Protestants. He chose 3 men to organise and to run the council: the future Pope Julius III; the future Pope Marcellus II, and an *Englishman,* Cardinal Reginald Pole (1500-1558.)

In 1549 Reginald Pole missed the statutory two-thirds majority by two votes to follow Pope Paul III, and to almost become the second English Pope in history: an ardent reformist, he was the leader of the 'Spirituali,' a group of clerical and lay thinkers, who were pushing Counter Reformation in the Roman Catholic Church. An influential figure during the 'English' Reformation, Reginald had been a Vatican emissary to the Tudors. Unfortunately, his ideas, which were felt to be controversial in the Vatican, led him to be sidelined by his arch rival, the conservative, 80 year-old, Neapolitan Cardinal, Pietro Caraffa,

INTRODUCTION

after he was elected Pope Paul IV. Caraffa had no confidence in the Council of Trent, and, from 1555 to 1559, broke the back of counter reform by rigorously applying the Roman 'Index' and sponsoring the 'Tribunal of the Inquisition.'

The Counter-Reformation was forced to await the pontificate of Pope Pius IV in 1560 before continuing: he made a belated, but comprehensive, effort to finalise the Council of Trent, which was finally brought to a close (after 21 years) in 1563. The Reformation itself did not run its course until the close of the Thirty Years' War, with the Peace of Westphalia in 1648. The trauma had taken 131 years to heal, during which time, schism, recrimination, martyrdom, heresy and apostasy had cleaved European Christianity.

Historical speculation is never wise, but for those who might have wished for a more pragmatic and less painful conclusion to the turmoil, it is hard not to regret that an immensely probable potential English pope was not given the chance by Rome to calm the choppy, Northern European waters by profiting from his cultural advantage: he already was a reformist, he was pragmatic, talented, and no doubt suitably *ironic* and *phlegmatic* too! At least he very probably suffered from a narrower cultural divide than an 80 year-old, conservative, Neapolitan pope in Rome's disastrous attempt to deal with the Germanic princes and the English Reformation.

Today's cultural supermen must surely be the Members of the European Parliament: take the little Anglo-French, cross-channel gap and multiply it across the growing number of Nordic, Saxon, Celtic, Gallic, Hispanic, Baltic, Latin, Germanic, Hellenic, Slavic, etc. countries, and we are justified in wondering whether the creation of a united Europe will be concluded in "two shakes of a lamb's tail:" waiting time has slid into a third generation – do you remember what Grandfather used to say about Europe? Our cultural differences, today, be they rooted in Rousseau's writings, or in the Magna Carta, or in Machiavelli's "Prince," or in the alleged capitalist consequences of Calvinism, or in the alleged

MACHIAVELLI AND THE MAYFLOWER

Roman distrust of lucre, go further, in my view, to enrich Europe's heritage rather than to inflame it. "Vive la difference," I say! But Europeans remain nonetheless flummoxed by the behaviour and attitudes of their cousins.

I have lived some years in the United States, and I love this vibrant, Christian republic with its pioneering roots and principles rooted in the Mayflower spirit, but the words *Christian*; *republic*; *Mayflower*, and the *pioneers* themselves, all originated in Europe.

Imagine a dinner in the Mid Western United States attended by 500 international executives of a large American corporation; 9-11 is still a burning memory, and there is universal sympathy in the room between trans-Atlantic friends. Tables of ten are made up; imagine sitting across from the Moslem president of a Pakistani subsidiary and the Taoist boss of one of the Chinese plants. Elsewhere in the room there are Hindus from India, and various Jewish colleagues from a dynamic Israeli subsidiary. At the start of the dinner, a fast tracking, corporate executive, who is a practicing Christian, walks up to the microphone, asks everyone to stand, and, without another word, plunges into a full blown *Christian* grace. Would the shock on the faces of all around this international table not be terrible to behold?

This type of scenario disturbs me enough to try to come up with an explanation of how well meaning persons can make what I believe to be blunders of this type. Would they find their roots in naivety or in bigotry, or lack of knowledge? It is the risk of this kind of event, and I have witnessed something similar, that has led me to think more about cultural difference, and to write this book.

A few points of order about what follows:
§   I take the word *culture* to mean common behaviours and attitudes of people located in the same geography: it does not refer to the many art forms which accompany the phenomenological human experience.

INTRODUCTION

§   The word *republican* is not intended to refer to the ideas of the United States political party of the same name: it refers to a political ideal of ancient Greek origin bent into shape by the writings of Thomas Hobbes, Jeremy Bentham, Jean-Jacques Rousseau and others.

§   I make no apology for following a 'Cartesian' structure in this book, where I start at what I perceive to be the beginning, then advance in what I hope to be acceptable explanation, and don't stop until I arrive at what I perceive to be the end: I think it best to spend the first chapters on laying the groundwork of religious and political basics as I see them before discussing resulting behaviour, as I see it; only then do I get around to a model for predicting behavioural and attitudinal stereotypes. For the *"cut the horse fluff, and don't waste my time"* approach, I'm afraid there's no executive summary.

§   I contrast Britain and France often in the pages that follow: this does not only arise from my reasonable level of 'comfort' with both cultures, but also, as the reader will discover, from the fact that these countries illustrate the two most important *extremes* of European culture as I see them, a predominantly *protestant monarchy*, and a predominantly *Roman Catholic republic*.

§   The largest country in Europe is Germany, which sits at the crossroads of European cultures, with its national balance, but regional imbalance, between Protestantism and Roman Catholicism; I do not speak of Germany enough, but I have extensively quoted one of its most eminent sons, Max Weber and built a part of my essay on his thesis. I would have liked to speak more of Scandinavia, of Spain, of the Benelux countries, and apologise for not having done so. At the end of the essay, I have however used the remarkable work of the eminent Dutch sociologist, Gerd Hofstede, as an empirical basis against which to validate some of my own.

§   Finally, I pay my respects at the outset to those theologians and philosophers who will have to put up with any half truths they discover: at some light years away from mastering their magnificent arts, I make no pretence of finding myself in their ranks.

MACHIAVELLI AND THE MAYFLOWER

AUTHOR'S FOREWORD TO THE FIRST EDITION

I have tried repeatedly during text revisions to find the correct words to express my opinions without giving offence; my only objective is to illustrate my idea of a hypothesised behavioural model and, if what I have made as statements of opinion about this model appear to the reader as statements of fact, this is totally unintentional; nothing in this book is intended to offend anyone. Generalisations about behaviour and attitudes are my personal opinions about behavioural caricatures as I imagine them, and about no individual; I believe that talking about them can promote mutual understanding and ultimately be in the public interest. When I cite the idea of *dysfunctional* behaviour and attitudes, this is to contrast certain thought processes that are in my view useful for understanding cultural differences and the way in which I believe they arise; they are not intended as judgements about individuals, nor about organisations, nor communities; I have only tried to apply the Confucian maxim quoted in the first lines of the Introduction.

The stereotypes described in Chapter 6 do not exist other than in my imagination, and any perceived resemblance to persons living or dead is purely coincidental.

Despite what I have said, if any remark I have made is perceived to give offence, or causes others to give offence, it should be rewritten: please be so kind as to inform my publisher and I will rewrite the offending passage for future editions.

Bob Gillespie, Paris, January 2009

CHAPTER 1

POLITICS AND RELIGION

...religion and politics have the same purpose among men; it is simply that, at the birth of nations, the one serves as the instrument of the other... Religion, considered in connection with societies, whether general or particular, can be divided into two categories, the religion of the man and the religion of the citizen.
Jean-Jacques Rousseau: The Social Contract

The roots of Western European culture grip deep into corridors of time, through generations of men and women, who have adjusted their behaviour to the political and religious prejudice of their times and learned to live in a harmony of shared values. Weather, living conditions, poverty and hunger may dictate national behaviour, but probably more European men and women have killed each other under the banners of politics and religion down through the ages than any other: the growth of a middle class, abundant food and a temperate climate, distinguish *politics* and *religion* as the critical drivers of collective European behaviour: they find their source in the classical political philosophy of the Greek city states; in the 3rd-century, neo-Platonic, and 12th-century, Aristotelian, metaphysics of the Roman Church, and in the consequent 16th-century sledgehammer of the Reformation.

The Greeks of antiquity developed the republican model of the city state in reaction to individual, despotic power, and discovered a unifying force within society which no longer resided in the will of tribal chiefs, but in laws promulgated through collective debate by, and for, the community. Debate required the use of reasoning and of rhetoric if the individual was to convince, and rational thought and presentation became the tools that allowed individuals to manage society effectively.

Rome took the Greek model and applied it to its expanding, multiethnic empire, and, around this backbone, the strength of the fledgling Roman Church grew throughout those years that the Italian 14th century playwright, Petrarch, dubbed, "The Dark Ages." During that period, the Church established both its spiritual and temporal power throughout Europe and remained unchallenged until, thanks to Arab intellectuals, the empirical philosophy of Aristotle appeared in new institutions of lay learning, called the "universitates," the first of which was in the Vatican's back yard, the Emilian city of Bologna. The effect was to put the abstract philosophy of Plato, up to then heavily drawn upon by the Church fathers, in its place using the practical thinking of his pupil, Aristotle. In consequence, at the turn of the millennium, under the impulse of Gregory the Great, the Roman Church shifted its focus away from neo-Platonism to improved understanding of this world, and Gregorian reform gave a new impulse to learning; a new idea appeared that salvation might also be won through the works of man, and not just through the merits of grace.

This enlightenment mutated heavily after the Renaissance and opened the floodgates to the upheaval of the 16th century Reformation, the thrust of which was to question a wide swath of Roman dogma, which had been founded on the teaching of the early fathers, and to challenge the temporal power in Rome: the Reformers set out to champion the less dogmatic, "this-worldly" view of Christianity.

Throughout the second millennium, Europe was governed by paternalistic and clannish leaders supported by military strength and justified though heredity: with the support of the Church, they transformed their power structures into medieval feudal monarchies and principalities. Ordinary men and women lived for centuries dependent upon the interests of such powerful individuals, and they collectively developed behaviours and attitudes geared to preserving the wealth and power of their prince, and so, to their own survival and to that of their families. The vast majority of society lived and worked under a dual bond of political loyalty to a feudal overlord and of religious submission to the Church, those two important vectors of development of behaviour and attitudes interacting with each other from the very beginning of European history.[2] In addition to *political* argument then, this book debates the effects of *religion* on behaviour, and, to try to avoid doctrinal disputes, I have coined two 'para-religious' terms: *Romanists* to denote people, whether they be Catholic or not, having behaviour or attitudes, functional or dysfunctional, which I believe find their origin in Catholicism; *Reformists* for those whose behaviour and attitudes appear to me to arise from *Calvinist* Protestantism, whether they be protestant or not: consequently, a Dutch, British or American Catholic could probably show more Reformist behavioural traits and attitudes than an Italian or Spanish Catholic because the Dutch, British and Americans have grown up in societies dominated by 'Reformist' behaviour. Equally, a long-term, British expatriate to Italy or to Spain, having acquired a distinctly Romanist outlook, may shock his Reformist counterparts on his return to Britain with his "foreign" behaviour. I do wish to affirm at the outset that my word Romanism does not mean *not* Roman Catholicism, and my word Reformism does not mean *not* Protestantism. These two words are chosen to describe a form of stereotypical behaviour and not religious doctrine or sensitivities.

I have chosen Calvinist Protestantism to illustrate Reformist ideals, (thanks in particular to the seminal work of Max Weber, the early controversial 20th century German sociologist, who showed that the origins of Capitalism are probably rooted in attitudes and behaviour originating in Calvinist Protestantism,) for

---

[2] Christianity preaches only servitude and submission. Its spirit is too favourable to tyranny for tyranny not to take advantage of it. True Christians are made to be slaves; they know it and they hardly care; this short life has too little value in their eyes.
Jean-Jacques Rousseau: The Social Contract

its stronger contrast with Catholicism than Lutheranism or Anglicanism. The Lutheran doctrine of justification by faith challenges Calvin's idea of Predestination, as does the umbilical chord linking Anglo Catholicism to Roman Catholicism, and for these reasons, ascetic Calvinism provides the greater mismatch with Roman doctrine. The founding fathers, who fled Plymouth on The Mayflower to establish their community in New England, were Puritans tarred with the stick of ascetic Protestantism: that their thoughts and customs should have underpinned today's American capitalism is wholly credible.

Two *political* models have left their marks on Western European attitudes: *feudal monarchy* and *republic*. Except for Switzerland and San Marino, feudal monarchy was virtually the only functioning model of state in Europe for a thousand years, so almost all Europeans have a feudal 'gene' in their 'constitutional DNA.' The French revolutionaries of 1789 led the way in Europe to the birth of a new republican state following the example of their American counterparts, who saw the road to independence from the British crown in their model of republican revolution: England had seen a republic during Cromwell's ten years in power and had rejected it, but after her return to monarchy, she lost her American colonies to the republican ideal. In both cases of feudal monarchy in France and of constitutional monarchy in Britain, princes were to pay the price of the republic in the loss of royal heads, power and wealth.

No political writer had better formulated the procedures that ensure the protection and the survival of monarchs than a contemporary of Martin Luther, Niccolò Machiavelli (1469-1527,) in his book 'The Prince.' He wrote this work while he was a diplomat posted by the humanistic Florentine republic to the court of the crafty Cesare Borgia, who was the son of Pope Alexander VI and Duke of the Roman Papal State, Romagna. The return of Florence with the support of the Vatican to its feudal, De Medici, overlords led Machiavelli to "turn his coat" and to dedicate his book to his new princely bosses while Italy observed in awe the systematic isolation and destruction of Cesare Borgia by his rival, the new Pope, Clement VII, otherwise called, Julius *De Medici*! It would appear that the Vatican had taken its eye off the ball, because the Reformation exploded while the Borgias and the De Medici were playing power politics. Machiavelli's outrageous scholarship, learnt in the night of medieval Rome, stands out as the definitive survival guide for kings and princes, but his wisdom interests us here primarily because his ideas are germane to understanding *individualism*, and of how it functions within European society.

The writings of Jean-Jacques Rousseau, and to some extent, of the anti-clerical Voltaire, set the model for the "modern" constitutional republic. Another outrageous thinker at a time when the French monarchy had been financially weakened by international adventure, Rousseau's thoughts inspired a hungry crowd in 1789 to wrest power from the ancient royal House of France and to place it in the hands of a popular meritocracy. Thomas Paine, heavily influenced by Rousseau, published his work, "Common Sense," in 1776, and set the wheels in motion for the fledgling American state to oust the British crown from America, ironically enough, with the help of the *French crown*, which fell from the French king's head shortly before that same head fell from the French king's body![3]

Probably better locked into the concepts of *equality* and *fraternity* than the Americans, the French have a different definition of *liberty*. If, today, the American constitution extols the principle of individual freedom, as found in the freedom in certain states to carry a gun, or in the freedom to conclude bank loans that are so risky as to lead to the collapse of some of Wall Street's most admired investment banks; French liberty is understood as the freedom of the collective from the power of a feudal monarch, as occurred during the French Revolution.

---

[3] There is something exceedingly ridiculous in the composition of monarchy; it first excludes a man from the means of information, yet empowers him to act in cases where the highest judgement is required. The state of a king shuts him from the world, yet the business of a king requires him to know it thoroughly.
Thomas Paine: Common Sense

European republicans identify their political ideals with modernism, but, in view of the pervasiveness of *constitutional* monarchy in Europe, is the Republic really more modern? Opinions die hard, however, and France, for example, continues to offer the fertile soil of political zeal to the supporters of collectivism in the cause of modernity.

Behaviour may vary between individuals, and from country to country, but European stereotypes, floating on a "froth" of centuries of functional and dysfunctional political and religious behaviour, continue to glare at each other across national frontiers. The chapters that follow make an attempt to explain those cultural gaps, beyond language, between European, whose forefathers did not submit to the same feudal overlords nor practise the same forms of Christianity; gaps which have caused civil war, terrorism and countless deaths. Not so long ago, people in Ireland were murdering each other under the banner of religious differences; their ancestors have fought each other since the 16th century, when post-Reformation religious war in Europe was the world's most destructive international conflict. The Irish were not alone in their religious violence: Europe saw thirty years of wars of religion in France leading to the St Bartholomew's Day massacre of the Huguenots; the execution of thousands of Dutch Protestants by the Duke of Alba sent by the Spanish king Philip II; the, albeit unsuccessful, Armada; the calamitous Thirty Years war between the German Palatinate and the Bavarian Catholic League, probably the most destructive conflict seen in Europe before the 1914-1918 Great War; the English Reformation, which saw martyrdom both in the Catholic and in the Anglican camps; and, of course, the Irish battle of the Boyne, which opposed James Stewart II of England with his son in law, William of Orange.

At the root of such violent behaviour lie political and religious intolerance; I believe that, if we could better understand *why* people of other cultures behave differently from us, we may feel less affronted when their reactions don't correspond with what we expect; greater understanding on our part could lead to greater tolerance of others who are not like us, and possibly make our world a little safer to live in. This is a hope I place in this essay.

So, down which lanes of thought should we amble to understand European behaviours? Is there a model to help us to predict cultural stereotypes in this diverse mass of peoples, who speak so many different languages in such a small part of our planet, and whose history has at times dominated global events in the Western hemisphere? There have been countless attempts to classify European behaviour and attitudes, but none convinces me more than the analysis of religious and political stereotypes.

But first, how shall we define Europe itself? Is this collection of diverse countries the political brainchild of Charlemagne, called by the French and the Germans, "The Father of Europe," or is it not rather just an agglomeration of peoples having borders in common? Historians have accepted both ideas with perhaps rather more emphasis placed on the dynamics of the shared cultures of Jerusalem and Athens: Jerusalem because the final acceptance of the Old Testament into the Christian Bible at the Synod of Hippo in 393 A.D. confirmed Christianity, (heavily influenced by St Augustine,) in the line of the Jewish faith; Athens because twelve centuries of classical Greek thought to some extent balanced the influence of faith with the influence of reason. Rome formed the hub around which such faith and reason were geographically transmitted throughout Christendom, which then included Byzantium, the door of the Orient: but Byzantium never really belonged to this concept of Europe, so Europe is held in this essay to be the post schismatic, pre-Reformation, Roman Catholic geography of Christendom.

Since the Renaissance, Europe has not only been transformed by *political* conquest, occupation and revolution, but also by *religious* Reformation, and this change has occurred *within* the area of Europe as it is geographically defined here. I am indebted to Professor Rémi Brague, whose book, 'Eccentric Culture,' well explains this reasoning, but there is no doubt that Europeans are predominantly   Christian,   and,   despite   Professor   Brague's approach of reducing most of European culture to its Jewish and Greek roots, I believe that the focus of a millennium of Roman Catholic religious monopoly with its attendant antithesis of the Reformation is the primary driver of European culture as we live it today: this is not to question the heritage of the Old Testament nor the seminal work of the Greek philosophers, it is more to relegate them both to their true perspective of antiquity, and to surface European Christianity, with its doctrinal content and religious guidance, as the more contemporary and appropriate influence. Professor Brague's thesis that the Roman Empire brought little more than administrative talent to our forefathers is to forget that the extraordinary institution of the Roman Catholic Church grew thanks to it, and that it has survived two millennia in accordance with Christ's promise to his apostle, Peter, the first Pope, appointing *him* the "rock" on which His Church was built. Professor Brague insists that Europe is defined by the Jewish Pentateuch, and by Plato's and Aristotle's metaphysics, but he overlooks in my view the influence of the Roman and protestant Churches.

There can be surely no doubt that Christianity is the most relevant and powerful driver of European culture through its Catholic and Protestant theologies. As Islam re-establishes a grip on Europe through the Turks in Germany, the North Africans of the Maghreb in France, the Pakistanis in Britain, or the Albanians in Italy, I have no doubt that its impact on European behaviour and attitudes will be just as determinative for *future* generations. For now, however, at the turn of the third millennium, I believe I can firmly stick my neck out and affirm that *Christianity* is *the* key historical religious vector in Europe.

The inertia of ideals in society is such that many generations must pass before they can be recognisably attributed to a contemporary philosophical line: we have no problem in recognising Plato's influence or Aristotle's, but how far do we recognise the influence of recent thinkers such as Wittgenstein, or Schopenhauer, Kant, Kierkegaard or Heidegger? It takes time for ideas to filter through to the practice of every day life, and we are still digesting the ideals of two millennia of Catholicism, half a millennium of Reformation and a quarter of a millennium of republican revolution.

European constitutional systems have in fact polarised themselves around two models, monarchy and republic. Early monarchy took a feudal form, protecting the absolute power of a ruler, but, as the Magna Carta has shown, good government led to the more democratic form of *constitutional* monarchy, paradoxically, better guaranteeing monarchical survival if not monarchical power. The Republic, which seems better suited to the various philosophies of collectivism, has developed from the oligarchic city states of antiquity to contemporary models with constitutional government and an elected president, be they democratic and liberal, as France, Germany or Italy, or not, as the now defunct Soviet Union or the National Socialist states of the 1920's and 1930's.

I have chosen these two axes to form a framework against which to categorise European behaviour and attitudes. One axis extends from the pole of Roman Catholicism to the other of Protestant Calvinism, and the other extends from Monarchy to Republic. I believe that we can categorise national behavioural stereotypes according to where their centre of gravity falls on such a grid. In this way, I would expect to find common behaviour and attitudes between countries that fall in the same section. Otherwise said, similarities exist between Catholic republics; other similarities exist between protestant monarchies; the same can then be said of the less prevalent European Catholic monarchies or protestant republics.

Most other cultural predictors seem to me to be secondary. I have heard that the weather can determine behavioural stereotypes, and while I don't dispute this, whereas men and women have killed each other on account of politics and religion down through the ages, I know of no case of anyone having been slaughtered on account of the weather, although I understand that the long, dark

Scandinavian winters can affect behaviour![4] No doubt poverty, living conditions, and hunger are also drivers, but I have not tried to integrate these ideas in this essay.

The next four chapters summarise arguments and historical events that I believe determine attitudes and behaviour of those who have grown up and live, respectively, in Romanist, Monarchical, Reformist and Republican societies. The book goes on to summarise stereotypes or behavioural caricatures that I believe such societies induce; finally, it goes on to describe the synergy that would be expected of mixing each political dimension with each religious one and the models that we can deduce.

---

[4] I recently discovered in analysing six centuries of data giving the first date each year of the Burgundy wine harvest, that 1793, the year of 'la Terreur,' when Louis XVI was finally collared by Robespierre, marked the end of the 30 coldest summers in French climatic history since 1370; it was the nadir of a mini ice age beginning in the early 18th century and ending with our current years of global warming. Could this indicate that, had the summers been warm and the harvest plenty, France would still be a monarchy?

CHAPTER 2

ROMANISM

Communion and excommunication are the social compact of the clergy, one through which they will always be masters of both people and kings. All the priests...are fellow citizens...This invention is a masterpiece of politics.
Jean-Jacques Rousseau: The Social Contract

The Roman Catholic Church traces its origins back 2,000 years to the times of Christ's apostles; the Roman Empire assisted its development throughout its growth, starting in the third century and continuing through the decline of Rome in the fifth, and, from the times of Charlemagne and of the Crusades, the Church tightened its grip over the European feudal monarchies, which were the only effective arms of geographical administration and power.

As the Roman 'Pontiff,' the Pope has monarchical status, and his influence in the political affairs of Europe has been determinant through the ages. Catholicism almost single-handedly shaped European ethics until the Reformation in the sixteenth century, testifying not only to the remarkable effectiveness of the Church's temporal organisation but also to the massive following of its faithful.

St. Irenaeus (ca. 130 – 202,) who was the Bishop of Lyons in the second century, faced with the multiplicity of Gnostic texts on the life of Christ, worked under the guidance of Rome to identify the scriptural writings that would be kept concerning His life and teaching, and to incorporate them into a 'New Testament.' The Christian Bible includes also an 'Old Testament,' which, in addition to the five books of Moses of the Jewish Torah, include, in the Catholic version, more recent Jewish texts, the Apocrypha. The Church fathers developed the Bible this way despite the resistance of Marcion of Sinope, who rejected any Hebrew content. Today's Bible, is thus, in a sense, *of* the Roman Church, (although the choice of books in the protestant Bible is different.) As the Church claims it has been invested with the divine mission of revealing God's plan for salvation to His faithful, the Roman Catholic Church would claim to stand, itself, at the centre of revelation *and not the Bible.* Within Roman Catholicism, the biblical texts mark one, but *not the only*, stage in the *ongoing tradition of revelation* by God to His faithful.[5]

Not long after healing the first divergence that separated the visions of St Paul and of St John, the early doctors of the Church defined the nature of doctrine and of heresy. Their intellectual tradition has continued down through the ages to recent theologians such as Pierre Teilhard de Chardin, a visionary French Jesuit, who held that all of creation is continually *working out* its salvation through Christ in a scientifically evolutionary sense, and whose ideas are still being considered by the Vatican more than five decades after his death.

The Church not only took its material from the Jewish books, which have evident links to New Testament scripture, but also from the writing of St Paul of Tarsus. His texts open onto the metaphysics of Plato, who lived some 400 years *before* Christ. Plato had already distinguished a *soul (psyche)* from the body (*empsucha*) and identified the 'self' with the soul, which he thought to be *immortal*, developing his ideas through the words of Socrates, of whom he wrote in the 'Phaedo.' He saw the soul as part of a *cosmic* force *imprisoned* in the body and resisting its *corrupt* desires. Death would *release* the soul from the body, and

---

[5] As a result the Church, to whom the transmission and the interpretation of Revelation is entrusted, "does not derive her certainty about all revealed truths from the holy Scriptures alone. Both Scripture and Tradition must be accepted and honoured with equal sentiments of devotion and reverence."
Catechism of the Catholic Church #82

the soul would be *rewarded* for virtue or *punished* for wickedness. Plato was admired and extensively quoted by Plotinus, St Anselm and St Augustine: his thought heavily influenced the Church during the first millennium until its rediscovery of Plato's pupil, Aristotle. Less quoted were Plato's ideas on reincarnation and homosexuality.

The writings of Aristotle were lost to early Christendom but conserved by Arab scholars and reintroduced through them into the Church at the end of the first millennium. Aristotle's empiricism supported a less mystical approach than Plato's metaphysics and was met with scepticism by the Vatican, however, by the time that St Thomas Aquinas (1225 – 1274,) one of the "Doctors of the Church," wrote his 'Summa Theologiae, Questions on God,' Aristotle was very much in vogue indeed. Aquinas makes over one hundred references to Aristotle in this work, and only ten or so to Plato.

The Church finally drew its *tradition* from both of these philosophers. There is a vast fresco called, 'The School of Athens,' painted by Raphael on one wall of the Vatican Library of Julius II showing Plato holding his Socratic dialogue, 'The Timaeus,' and pointing his index finger upwards; Aristotle is holding his 'Ethics' and pointing outwards: their gestures are intended to portray Plato focussed on abstract and theoretical principles, and Aristotle attempting to understand the world around us. That fresco, which appears on the cover of this book, richly evokes the competition between mysticism and empiricism which would be illustrated in the rift between Catholicism and Protestantism.

The Roman Catholic Church's position on biblical authority is not just far removed from that of the protestant fathers of the Reformation, who take the Bible as the sole and definitive revelation by God to His faithful, but is even in considerable contradiction with it. The differences in attitudes and behaviour induced by such a theological gap throw into contrast the cultural vectors of dogmatic Catholicism with those of pragmatic

Protestantism. The mystical teaching of Catholicism is assimilated on faith by a following that relies upon revelation preached under priestly guidance as the ultimate authority of God's word, rather than on a possibly more private search for truth in the Bible in line with protestant practice. [6]

Roman Church doctrine is founded on many platforms, such as Plato's concept of the soul and of life after death; on the work of Irenaeus in choosing which books to integrate into the New Testament, including St. Paul's 'Platonic' writings; on the rejection of the Gnostic Gospels; on the choice of the Pentateuch and of the Apocrypha for the Old Testament; and on the later discovery of the work of Aristotle, all further interpreted by 'doctors' of the church, such as, St Augustine (Plato,) St Thomas Aquinas and Duns Scotus (Aristotle.) The Pope proclaims dogmatic truth speaking 'Ex Cathedra,' not just on the basis of these writings, but also on that of 'Tradition,' a concept justified by Aristotle's idea of 'reputable opinion.' All such 'truths' are taught to the faithful by priests, whose own faith has been reinforced, and whose own thinking has been moulded, by long years of training and prayer. Tradition incorporates far more than the Bible and has evolved over the centuries. The weight of tradition leads the Romanist to take it for granted that the past is indispensable for understanding the complexities of the present; not for him Henry Ford's famous remark that "History is bunk!"

As many philosophers are still struggling with the problem of free will and determinism, and do not even appear to be convinced by the four major arguments for the existence of God, [7] the Roman faithful necessarily accept priestly teaching including traditional

---

[6] "The task of giving an authentic interpretation of the Word of God, whether in its written form or in the form of Tradition, has been entrusted to the living, teaching office of the Church alone. Its authority in this matter is exercised in the name of Jesus Christ. This means that the task of interpretation has been entrusted to the bishops in communion with the successor of Peter, the Bishop of Rome.
Catechism of the Catholic Church #85

[7] The Ontological, Cosmological, Teleological arguments and the argument from Eternal Truths.

teaching not in the Bible, on faith, knowing that such fundamental premises cannot be substantiated by empirical enquiry.

The mystical idea of God is common to all Christianity, both for Catholics and for Protestants, however, unlike Protestantism, the ongoing evolution of Catholic dogma beyond any idea of a single definitive biblical revelation implies further leaps of faith each time that papal infallibility is invoked.

I call the thought process by which people internalise mystical claims on faith alone, "elliptic."[8] Elliptic thought rationalises paradox by making, for example, un-provable ideas, or ones in apparent contradiction with empirical data, credible; elliptical construction leaves uncertainty unsaid, assumes premises on faith alone, and gives equivalent weight to theory and to synthesis as it does to fact and to evidence; it helps to construct on faith without 'this worldly' proof of essential premises; it stems from, and reinforces, the conviction that 'truths' are *not* plain and simple; it encourages tolerance for argument on more artistic and creative planes than logic, but it provokes a 'flight' to Cartesian scepticism and to deductive logic, as if pedantry could compensate the strain that elliptic thought puts on the mind.

Pre-Roman literature gives three meanings to the word "elliptic:" *defective* (Theognis; Plato; Lysias; Eustatius); *incomplete* (Plotinus), and *falling short* (Aristophanes; Aristotle; Polybius.) The contemporary sense is: an *incomplete expression*; a phrase *lacking a word or words needed to complete the sense* of the sentence; *leaving something out*; *to be understood*; *intentionally lost* or obfuscated; arriving at a *conclusion without delineating its steps*.

Ellipsis may be the antechamber to the *numinous* awe felt in the presence of the Almighty. Numinous is the term coined by German theologian Rudolf Otto to describe that which is *wholly*

---

[8] ...all attempts to make a purely speculative use of reason in reference to theology are entirely fruitless and of their inner nature, null and void.
Immanuel Kant: Critique of Pure Reason

other. It is the *'mysterium tremendum et fascinans'* that leads to
belief in deities, the supernatural, the sacred, the holy, and the
transcendent. It can be considered as that "intense feeling of
unknowingly knowing that there is something which cannot be
seen." Such "knowing" can overcome a person with feelings of
awe, as one might feel in a cathedral; next to a silent stream; on a
lonely road; early in the morning, or in watching a lovely sunset.
The word is equally applied to the sensation of fright experienced
in sensing the presence of evil, such as a ghost or an evil spirit.
The word was used by the Lutheran theologian, Rudolph Otto, in
his book *Das Heilige* (1917,) and was an important concept in the
writings of Carl Jung and of C. S. Lewis. The numinous is an
important component of catharsis, a powerful emotion which can
be experienced in the practice of the sacraments.

The position of the Roman Church on salvation is considerably
more optimistic than that of Jean Calvin, who gloomily concluded
that certain individuals are irretrievably predestined from all time
to damnation. Calvin found no other possible logical solution to
the paradox of the joint existence of hell and of a good God than
that of binary damnation or salvation known to God from all
eternity for every individual. Does inevitable damnation to hell
for some beings equate with a human concept of God's infinite
benevolence? Calvin set out to look for an answer;[9] Chapter 4
describes what he found.

Until the 16th century, European kings and their subjects relied
exclusively on Roman authority and doctrine to point the road to
Paradise: in so doing, they placed their faith in Church teaching.
Such acceptance of Church ascendancy in matters of faith
implicitly establishes an authoritative relationship between the

---

[9] Chapter III (of God's Eternal Decree), No 3. By decree of God, for the manifestation of His
glory, some men and angels are predestined unto everlasting life, and others foreordained to
everlasting death.
Westminster Confession of 1647
...with His quite incomprehensible decrees (God) has decided the fate of every individual and
regulated the tiniest details of the cosmos from eternity.
Max Weber: The Protestant Ethic and the Spirit of Capitalism

priests and the faithful that would appear to resemble the one existing between a parent and a child.

The Roman Catholic priest is called "Father;" rather than playing the role of a 'physical' father towards his 'children,' the priest assumes that of a spiritual one under the Church's authority. Many of today's psychologists recognise the primary function of the father toward the child as protection and confidence building, and the expectation of the child from the father is advocacy with the all powerful, nurturing mother, who, in this case, could be said to be represented by the Church *herself*: the father's function is fundamental to the child's understanding of its placement within the family hierarchy and to the construction of its self esteem. The relationship between the priests and the faithful is based on this powerful, natural model; the teaching of the priests comforts and accompanies the faithful as they walk the road of life, hopefully, towards sanctity.

The Roman Church endorses the idea of the onward march of each individual soul, as indeed that of all creation, towards salvation: it asserts that, through grace obtained by virtue and good works, man can indeed use his free will to win salvation in an intrinsically virtuous material world. God's creation cannot be inherently bad: it is man's diabolical thoughts, words and deeds that are evil. The great challenge to this doctrine of the inherent goodness of creation was posed by the Cathars in the 13th century: they loathed this material world which they considered to be intrinsically evil: their 'Albigensian' heresy was suppressed by the Inquisition. At a time when Islam was advancing through Spain and threatening Southern Europe, heresy encouraged the Roman Church to tighten its grip, leading to unfortunate times and to the preparation of the region of Navarre in South Western France for the later seed of Huguenot Protestantism: the Roman clergy has always been attentive to heresy, and at times in its history, quite ruthless in its suppression.[10]

---

[10] An apostate from the faith, a heretic or a schismatic incurs a latae sententiae excommunication.....

In defending the idea that man does effectively exercise his free will in choosing to be virtuous or not, Roman Catholicism accepts that an infinitely good, omniscient and omnipotent God nevertheless allows some of His faithful to burn eternally in hell because they have chosen this destiny through their own free will. The ideas that man has free will and that he chooses his own fate for all eternity appear to clash with the idea of God's infinite goodness, infinite knowledge and infinite power: would he not choose to save each and every one of his billions of poor human creatures struggling down the same treacherous path of life to certain death?[11]

Catholicism extols the monastic life, which is held to transcend the demands of worldly existence through extreme asceticism, isolation and self denial. The Franciscan model developed by the example of its founder, St Francis of Assisi, is rooted in praise of poverty and of strength of the virtuous person through his or her humility in a world bearing the sanctifying stamp of the magnificence of God's creation. Catholicism takes such monastic poverty very seriously and fights against the "false idol" of money. Such teaching is firmly other-worldly: the seeming glorification of poverty and of child-like weakness in the New Testament image of the Beatitudes polarises the Roman Church against power and wealth: sanctity pertains to Paradise, and, to gain it, the faithful must remain indifferent to the power, money and comforts of this world. Man's condemnation to work is the outcome of Original Sin, and his employment concerns subsistence and not profit. Money is an idol: it is 'unclean,' and,

---

The term latae sententiae describes that penalty which is automatically incurred on committing an offence, without the intervention of a judge or Superior.
The Code of Canon Law: Canon #1364

[11] ...human actions...either can have no moral turpitude at all, as proceeding from so good a cause; or if they have any turpitude, they must involve our Creator in the same guilt, while He is acknowledged to be their ultimate cause and author...to defend absolute decrees and yet free the Deity from being the absolute author of sin, has been found hitherto to exceed all the power of philosophy.
David Hume: Enquiries concerning Human Understanding and concerning the Principles of Morals

within the hands of the unscrupulous individual, the tool of the devil.

The praise of monastic asceticism would show that it is but a short step to a Romanist conclusion that poverty, which is viewed as a scourge everywhere else, could be in a way admirable, and that, if poverty is close to sanctity, then there is no point in trying to "fix it."[12] Such thought would appear to be elliptical.

Financial success is suspect without the ethic to justify it that Max Weber describes. In France, the protestant Huguenot movement was hurt on St Bartholomew's Day, 24th August 1572, when the bells of St Germain l'Auxerrois in Paris rang out to give the signal to the Catholics to start massacring the Protestants in the capital; 26 years later, the protestant Henry IV calmed the waters with the Edict of Nantes promoting secularism and tolerance. The backbone of Protestantism was finally shattered once and for all when Henry's grandson, Louis XIV revoked the Edict in 1685 outlawing Protestantism and provoking the flight of the Huguenots from France to Prussia, Flanders, Britain and as far as South Africa; in doing so, Louis virtually ensured that the concept of the Protestant Work Ethic and its attendant justification of the accumulation of capital through virtuous work would be banished from French thought: it appears to remain absent to this day; *business* is frowned upon as not being an acceptable career for the children of gentlefolk, and the word[13] is even synonymous with crookedness.

Hence, Romanist behaviour implies distrust of money, and risks alienating the rich: it appears implicit that virtue and money don't mix, and rich Romanists may feel advised to dispossess themselves of their money or, in conscience, to give to the

---

[12] ....the greater other-worldliness of Catholicism, the ascetic character of its highest ideals, must have brought up its adherents to a greater indifference toward the good things of this world...Medieval ethics not only tolerated begging, but actually glorified it in the mendicant orders.
Max Weber: The Protestant Ethic and the Spirit of Capitalism

[13] French: "Les affaires"

Church, which is in need of funds to finance its vast ministry. St Paul comforts the Church's point of view and challenges the wealthy by claiming that material gain beyond personal needs is futile in a world that is passing away (1-Corinthians 7-31;) St. Luke lambasts riches in his gospel too (Ch 16 vs. 19-31:) as a consequence, within Romanist societies, money would tend to be hidden by those who have it;[14] the young are periodically reminded by priests of the gospel which compares getting a rich man into Heaven with that of getting "a camel through the eye of a needle." Is it not surprising that the rich Romanist understates his money, behaves with muted elegance and shuts up about it? However, as an institution, the historical Roman Church has always had to deal face to face with money; whether with the rich medieval Italian city states such as Venice and Genoa, or in exploiting its own Papal states, or in finding the enormous funds necessary to finance today's apostolic mission in this material world, it welcomes the inflow of funds in the name of God's work.

If money is a false idol that blocks the road to salvation, then the true path would lie through poverty and asceticism. The practice of asceticism is indeed admired by the Catholic faithful: it is a property of the monastic life, where individuals work out their salvation through chaste solitude, poverty, obedience and prayer, rather than through the hustle and bustle of every-day life. In the this-worldly sphere of the non-cleric, where a man or a woman does not follow the religious path of asceticism and self denial of the Catholic clergy; where he or she has to earn a living; where families need to be provided for, and where lack of money can be of obsessive concern, there can grow a suspicion that such standards set for sanctity may be unreasonably difficult to follow for the ordinary man or woman in the street: poverty may be close to sanctity, but it may seem more of an affliction to a poor family.

---

[14] L'embarras des richesses.
Abbé d'Allainval, 1726

There is a hint of elliptic thought in praising poverty, and, in my view, the seed of dysfunctional behaviour among the lay faithful. Such admiration of poverty appears also to be in contradiction with the Calvinist thought described by Max Weber, where, in this world, wealth is *bestowed* by God on the *virtuous* in the pursuit of His work. The ideal of a link between virtue and wealth was so influential and logically consistent that other protestant faiths, such as the Methodists, have at times espoused it too, but not without with the caveat of the sin to which wealth can lead.[15]

Although the possible excesses of the Inquisition have been consigned to the history books, the Catholic Church appears to severely punish heresy but to remain indulgent with the sinner. In the wake of post Vietnam-War liberalism and Pope John XXIII's Second Vatican Council, gone seem to be the sack cloth and ashes for the sinful layman. In fact, one of the vectors of ascendancy of the Church over its faithful, and one of its most powerfully cathartic, sacramental tools is the absolution of sin. A Roman Catholic, who sins, does so believing that the stain of sin can be removed from his soul if he takes the sacrament. Catholicism portrays a forgiving God, not only ready to wash away the Original Sin of mankind through baptism but also to provide through the ministry of His Church what mankind needs to clean up his daily sins too: such a road to grace seems infinitely more optimistic than the destiny taught by Calvin. The cathartic nature of Catholic sacramental forgiveness appears to supply a safety valve through which sinful humanity can "dust off the dirt" before accessing divine grace. The act of absolution, which is the priestly power to intervene on behalf of the Creator to forgive the individual's sin, reinforces the mystical content of the sacrament and provides an occasion for a cathartic gush of emotion: in this respect, it is an exceptionally powerful sacrament.

---

[15] For religion must necessarily produce both industry and frugality, and these cannot but produce riches. But as riches increase, so will pride, anger, and love of the world in all its branches...We ought not to prevent people from being diligent and frugal; we must exhort all Christians to gain all they can, and to save all they can; that is, in effect, to grow rich. *John Wesley: quoted in Southey, Life of Wesley*

Taken to its extreme, a *dysfunctional Romanist* might actually conclude that he or she could sin with impunity simply by seeking sacramental absolution. Salvation would appear available simply in following the sacramental rule, and elliptic thought would satisfy the *dysfunctional Romanist* that the moral life is necessarily subject to contradiction: for example, salvation could be won every time despite his or her sinfulness because sacramental procedure exists to forgive sin, and he or she would be saved from eternal damnation despite the seeming inaccessibility of the rules of Catholic virtue by the lay faithful, such as poverty, asceticism or sexual abstinence. *Dysfunctional Romanism* would appear to permit the believer to sin again and again and to win salvation despite his or her sinfulness; sin could appear to be an *expected* human condition, resolved through His Church by an infinitely forgiving God. Guided by the parable of the Prodigal Son, the Church might even seem to make a welcoming fuss of the repentant sinner!

Dysfunctional Romanist spirituality would thus imply a cycle of sin, repentance, forgiveness, atonement, and renewed sin, all in the seeming absence of clerical hostility, at least since Vatican II.[16] Of course, this view of the sacrament of penance is certainly not the teaching or practice of Catholicism, which must include the firm intention to avoid further occasions of sin and atonement in the sacrament; this is why we speak here of *dysfunctional Romanist* behaviour, and *not* of the Roman Catholicism itself.

How different this is from the Calvinist extreme, where sin is specifically the property of the eternally damned, who can do nothing to save themselves from their predestined path to hell. The sinner is an 'untouchable,' and the pious, 'called' Calvinist will leave him, be he a beggar or the President of a nation, in no doubt about that. The characteristic of the Calvinist position is its humanly logical consistency, but it is an arduous line to follow,

---

[16] It might be true that the dark confessional is in some ways responsible for the habitual impunity of Italian society, but it's also, I thought, true that it contains an admirable sincerity. *Tobias Jones: The Dark Heart of Italy*

and gives no avenue of escape to the eternally damned. The Catholic notion of a forgiving God is infinitely less stressful, and, through the doctrine of Original Sin, shrugs off the question of how an all knowing, all powerful and all loving God allows his earthly children to misuse their free will to condemn themselves to eternal hell. The vestiges of Roman dogma retained in Anglicanism give birth to theological work which is as relevant to the Roman Catholic as to the Anglican: a prime example is found in the work of C.S. Lewis, whose extraordinary books, such as 'The Problem of Pain," or, "Mere Christianity," originally broadcast by the BBC, throw clear light onto, if not entirely resolving, the challenge of reconciling God's omnipotence, omniscience and omnibenevolence.[17]

In a religion where the standards for sanctity seem to be difficult to attain for the non cleric, where the sinner is said to be loved, and where God is assumed to be infinitely forgiving, a *dysfunctional Romanist* might rationally be led to consider himself, or herself, as a *loveable* sinner: he or she could break the Commandments and still find divine compassion as one of God's

---

[17] *On the Fall and Original Sin:*
What man lost by the Fall was his original specific nature...human spirit, from being the master of human nature became a mere lodger in his own house, or even a prisoner...a new kind of man - a new species, never made by God, had sinned itself into existence...Our present condition, then, is explained by the fact that we are members of a new species...I call our present condition one of Original Sin.
On God's Omniscience and man's free will illustrated by Abraham's 'trial,' when he was ordered to sacrifice Isaac
If God is omniscient He must have known what Abraham would do...But as St Augustine points out, whatever God knew, Abraham at any rate did not know that his obedience could endure such a command until the event taught him: and the obedience which he did not know that he would choose, he cannot be said to have chosen
On God's Omnipotence
...the ultimate loss of a single soul means the defeat of omnipotence. And so it does. In creating beings with free will, omnipotence from the outset submits to the possibility of such defeat. What you call defeat, I call miracle: for to make things which are not Itself, and thus to become, in a sense, capable of being resisted by Its own handiwork, is the most astonishing and unimaginable of all the feats we attribute to the Deity.
[17]*On God's Omnibenevolence to fallen man and the doctrine of hell*
What are you asking God to do?" To wipe out their past sins and, at all costs, to give them a fresh start, smoothing every difficulty and offering every miraculous help? But he has done so, on Calvary. To forgive them? They will not be forgiven. To leave them alone? Alas, I am afraid that is what He does.
C.S. Lewis: The Problem of Pain

beloved, weak and sinful creatures. "I may be a sinner, but I'm forgivable and soon forgiven, so why worry?" Such a man might see himself as mischievous, lovable and child-like doing forgivable wrong; he would believe that the sin cannot be confused with the sinner; one may be abhorrent, but the other is repeatedly salvageable: he could believe he can get away with anything, as a spoilt child might believe it. He would construct few internal barriers to doing wrong, and the tougher God of Moses would be conveniently forgotten; he might be led to believe that "anything goes." Despite its unyielding spiritual authority and dogmatism, the Roman Catholic Church appears exceptionally tolerant of the sinner; the *dysfunctional Romanist* might almost feel that the Church *expects* its faithful to be serial sinners.

In all events, if a dysfunctional Romanist does not discipline himself to be saved, he is ultimately dependent on the sacraments administered by the Church for his salvation. As the Church administers to the needs of his soul through the sacraments, salvation might almost appear as an *external* responsibility, that is, of the Church, rather than subject to his own individual free will. If the Church is invested with God's ultimate authority in matters of salvation, because sinful man cannot know salvation except through the Church, then he may conclude that he is more dependent on the Church and on its clergy than upon his own prayer and works for his salvation. He may thus feel that he could abdicate his spiritual condition to the responsibility of the Church, and come to believe that *external obedience* is sufficient to ensure his salvation. This would leave little need to attempt to personally attain values of virtue and piety through the asceticism held in such high esteem, not only by Calvinist Protestants, but also, in accordance with true Catholic teaching, by the thousands of religious and clergy of the Roman Catholic Church, and by the hundreds of millions of pious, *non-dysfunctional* lay faithful who do indeed lead the virtuous life the Roman Catholic Church encourages them to lead.

The *dysfunctional Romanist*, then, appears to play the role of a mischievous, spoilt child, dependent upon a clerical father figure, confident that *mother* Church will always support him as a particular, loveable, especially pardonable case and forever intervene with God on his behalf.[18] Is this idea not in stark contrast with Calvinist 'moral absolutism,' where individual circumstances can in no way bend *universal* ideals of right and wrong, without any tolerance whatever, at any time, under any circumstance?

The virtuous Catholic, like the virtuous Protestant, walks the path of life assuming he is going to fall into sin from time to time, but doing his level best to be virtuous, and, if a Catholic, using the sacraments in good faith. The *dysfunctional Romanist* believes that he can do whatever is *expedient* because he is going to be pardoned anyway: to him, the Calvinist might reply that, "you can't trick the Almighty, who has identified the sinner from all eternity." The cycle of sin, guilt, and cathartic pardon, leads the *dysfunctional Romanist* to justify sin through convenience and to *rationalise his guilt*. How does elliptic thought justify *dysfunctional Romanist* behaviour? The mental somersault is not hard to do and the following examples show how it might occur.

§   The clergy affirm that artificial birth control is immoral: well, you don't need five children any more to work the farm and you can't afford them anyway, so its reasonable to conclude that birth control is necessary in a world where sex is plastered all over the media; and anyway, the clergy is expected not to marry, so priests don't know what it is to get into bed every night with a partner: birth control is available, necessary, and everyone uses it, and you're forgiven anyway.

---

[18] Thus a true filial spirit towards the Church can develop among Christians. It is the normal flowering of the baptismal grace which has begotten us in the womb of the Church and made us members of the Body of Christ. In her motherly care, the Church grants us the mercy of God which prevails over all our sins and is especially at work in the sacrament of reconciliation. With a mother's foresight, she also lavishes on us day after day in her liturgy the nourishment of the Word and Eucharist of the Lord.
Catechism of the Catholic Church #2040

§   It's reasonable to expect sexual infidelity: sexual adventures happen to everyone; just look at the media! There's nothing wrong with a bit of mischief now and then, or even quite often, and you get forgiven anyway.

§   You're expected to turn the other cheek, but if the other guy's going to kill you, you're allowed to defend yourself; you can even kill in self defence or in a so-called 'just' war: so, at times, you don't need to turn the other cheek. It's tough to love when the other guy has just smacked you in the eye, and the Bible claims an eye for an eye: so, if it's not convenient to turn the other cheek, sometimes it's OK to whack the other guy back, and you get forgiven anyway.

§   There are so many circumstances where it can be convenient to lie, and, though lies are sinful, man is forgiven his sins anyway: lies are to be expected, so it's OK to lie.

§   The insurance company sends an inspector to check on a leak on the plumbing: a few weeks later he offers a reimbursement that you accept: then a survey from the insurance company enquires about your satisfaction over the arrangement, and you answer that you are dissatisfied, not because you are, but because on a matter of principle you are not going to admit it to the insurance company.

§   You are booking a holiday on a tropical island and you ask whether your choice of date is the right time of year for the weather; the tour operator knows it's the monsoon season, but tells you it's a great time to go, thinking it can't rain all day long, and that you should have checked for yourself on the Internet anyway. He doesn't care because it was a small lie and he needs the business, and he'll be forgiven anyway.

§   Owning up to wrongdoing leads to punishment of man by man, but the Romanist knows that man can only truly be forgiven by God for the wrong he has done, so there's no point in owning up to another man: you should therefore never own up or admit error to other men because forgiveness is divine and men are not divine: men cannot truly forgive. Vendetta is rational in human behaviour, so owning up only leads to punishment: owning up to other men is really naive and masochistic. It is OK not to own up, and you can get divine forgiveness anyway.

§   You've got to make a living: being rich is evil, but you can't reasonably expect anyone not to like money, and anyway, it's necessary for survival, and there's no reason the family should suffer over a medieval doctrine on poverty; money is a necessary evil: it is thus OK to have money, and you get forgiven for having it anyway, especially if you buy out your conscience by giving some to the Church.

§   It's reasonable to expect that rules can't always be followed: in fact rules are dangerous just because they can't always be followed. Because rules are never that simple to follow, the *dysfunctional Romanist* assumes that it is reasonable not to follow them; simplicity is an illusion; "yes" and "no" seem so often to lead to complication that they just don't matter; it's naïve to think that they do.

§   A child brought up in a poor environment is an innocent product of hardship, so it is understandable that he should in later life steal from others or exploit women on the street, because his anger is only human, and God, who sees into his soul, will pardon him anyway. He may lead a life of murder and extortion, but it's not his fault; it was his parents fault;' society's; the housing-project architect's; the schoolmasters,' etc.

The list goes on and on: elliptic thought can be used to justify just about anything. Of course, sin is evil, but sin can be pardoned and evil can be erased: it is at times convenient, even explainable, and can be committed with impunity because divine pardon is available; whatever happens, man can sin and be divinely forgiven. This is the recurring theme of *expediency* in *dysfunctional Romanist* behaviour. It is a short step from here to justifying to oneself a job in the Mafia or in the Camorra or in the 'Ndrangheta. Such thought processes reconcile binaries: no with yes; black with white; and right with wrong. Expediency is pervasive in Machiavellianism, as we shall see in a later chapter, and is light years removed from the morally absolutist, protestant platitude of "doing the right thing at all costs," which seems dear to American TV-soap script writers. *Dysfunctional Romanism* weakens the ideal of acting on principle: the behaviour of the "honourable" Victorian schoolboy, who owns up in front of the class to his peccadillo, would strike the *dysfunctional Romanist* as the height of naivety on the part of the schoolboy, and ridiculous over-reaction on the part of any schoolmaster, who expects him to own up: little boys would be expected to tell lies, and what the schoolmaster doesn't know, probably won't hurt him. Such attitudes seem prevalent on the roads in certain countries, where parking is at times chaotic, and where rules are not always respected by drivers; in such nations, cars are made with unpainted plastic bumpers because manufacturers know that a car parked in a city street will be jostled by drivers pushing bumper-to-bumper for parking space to get their own car in: it's only a little scratch; it can be painted over, and no one will notice. Try doing that in Zurich! *Dysfunctional Romanism* provokes catch-me-if-you-can tactics on the roads, and police behaviour probably more in line with teaching wrongdoers a lesson than with serving the community.

Such complacency explains dysfunctional Romanist bafflement with the seemingly exaggerated reactions of protestant societies towards the peccadilloes of their public people: many believe that powerful men and politicians have extra-marital sex and lie all the time; they think that this is what power and politics are all about: so what would make the inmate of the White House any different from that of any European presidential palace? How many Europeans remember a politician getting sacked for telling a lie? It might be assumed that most politicians lie repeatedly; as if they were almost expected to lie and as if expecting them not to do so, is absurd! Whoever heard of a politician without a regular hormone flush, anyway?

Comfort with paradox, where wrong can be right, leads the dysfunctional Romanist to reject the idea that only logical, simply expressed, linear, 'this worldly' statements are valid: God's logic is not human logic; creation is not plain or simple; simplicity is very probably a childish illusion. Romanist communication integrates complexity, and achieves this by being indirect, implicit, coded, circuitous, and elliptic. As a Romanist, when I say "no," perhaps I really mean that "it depends."[19]

Complexity requires the show of emotion to fully communicate the intricacy of human feelings: hiding feelings and not showing emotions can make other Romanists suspicious of deceit: they may assume that lack of visible emotion equates with lack of conviction or of sincerity. In a dispute, the Romanist is probably thinking, "Don't just say I'm wrong: persuade me; charm me; show me some emotion, so that my comfort level in believing you is higher!" Phlegm and the 'stiff upper lip' disorient him because of the 'disconnection' that appears between what the other man is saying and what his body, voice, face and hands are showing: little wonder he find might the patrician "Brit," who was taught from his earliest years to dissimulate emotion, 'perfidious,' and superficial. It is little wonder that phlegm frightens him and that irony escapes him, despite the nudge and the wink. It possibly explains why the only English Pope, ever, had difficulty in getting his point of view across to his Latin colleagues and why a medieval, English runner up to the Papacy couldn't completely convince a Neapolitan colleague of the need for a counter reformation. Non-verbal communication is essential to conveying complexity within Romanist cultures: facial and manual gestures and the use of body language are not just advisable, but necessary. The assumption of complexity requires knowing the complete man: you have to get in close: "Only trust a man," the

---

[19] For someone used to the whitewashed walls of Methodist chapels, where religion appears simple, cerebral, occasionally austere, and sometimes dull, the story of Catholicism and the Vatican in recent years appears completely the opposite: colourful, confusing, gripping and always mysterious.
Tobias Jones: The Dark Heart of Italy

Turks are reputed to say, "if you can smell his breath." Such types of interchange are termed *diffuse*: they require a wide range of expression between individuals for communication to succeed; within more pragmatic cultures, where relations can be perfectly functional in the absence of non verbal communications, the narrower basis for relationships is termed *specific*.

René Descartes, the French philosopher, was a fan of *deductive* logic: his form of discourse, termed 'Cartesian,' implies starting with an undisputed premise; questioning and examining each successive logical argument; convincing and securing agreement at every step before progressing to the next; taking obsessive care to use logical deduction to resolve objections *before* continuing; and building step by logical step until the ultimate goal of proof is achieved. What the French call, "Cartesianism," an efficient tool for discussing complexity in Romanist cultures, is judged painstaking, long-winded and unwieldy in pragmatic, time-saving Reformist societies, far more at home with *inductive* argument.[20]

Cartesianism blocks Romanist thought from so easily finding refuge in construction and puts energy into winning over opinion. It requires the individual to prove his point and to express it with philosophical elegance: as a result, meetings don't need to be conclusive and are frequently only called to verify the logical process or to poll opinion. The Romanist tends not to come to the point: he is more concerned with the process of using argument to ensure that others understand context; he expects every step of his idea to be sceptically questioned, and assumes that decisions can be dangerous if *all* facets of a problem are not thoroughly evaluated first. Because the Romanist mistrusts simplicity and linearity, Reformist inductive pragmatism does not attain his level of comfort. He takes nothing at face value: *if a solution is not complex, it probably is not a good solution.* In Romanist societies,

---

[20] Descartes seems to suggest that there can be an uninterrupted (*i.e. deductive*) chain of reasoning from the two principles of his metaphysics ("I am thinking, therefore I am" and "God exists.")
Tom Sorell: Descartes – A Very Short Introduction.

people do not do things because they have been told to, but because they have understood and elected to buy in. Cartesianism tolerates dissent, but its objective is consensus, and, at the outside, compromise, as the last resort when argument cannot finally be reconciled.

For deductive argument to be sound, the premises must be undisputed; but, is the fact that religious dogma is un-provable, and that its consequences are rigorously deduced in Cartesian fashion, not in itself elliptical? Descartes held that, if religious premises, such as the very existence of God, are taken on faith, then at least any deduction from them must be logically rigid: interestingly enough, this idea brings together Calvin and Aquinas: what really separates the two appears to be the number and complexity of the religious premises beyond biblical authority that constitute the tradition of Roman dogma. However, as much as debate is tolerated, the dogmatic behaviour of the Church discourages lay Romanists from thinking that they can reformulate or interpret doctrine: procedures and the written word are sacrosanct: you disregard the teaching of the Church at your peril.

Within a complex world, the Romanist *needs* to be qualitative. Quantitative, fact-based inductive argument lacks the richness necessary to communicate all the 'softer' facets of an issue. Romanist society delights in discussion and in an honest desire to resolve contradiction by using deductive logic: it is reasonable and necessary to debate and to discuss. Within the complexity of creation, nothing is what it seems, and debate serves to get a grip on what is hidden, and what is hidden can often only be treated qualitatively. Heightened sensitivity to what is hidden and to what is difficult to express other than quantitatively gives the Romanist consummate artistic flair; he suffers from no barriers to synthesising what cannot be proven to exist; there is nothing to hamper his creativity.

The Roman Church puts imperatives of time in a long term context: because time is eternal and the final coming of the

Redeemer always appears far into the future, the idea of *now* becomes unimportant on the scale of God's eternity. If the Romanist is doing something else, he may not feel it unreasonable to be late. Timekeeping can be unimportant in his society, and he is little disposed to cut business short on the sole principle of being on time; deadlines can be flexible and timekeeping unpredictable; agendas can float and appointments can be postponed, or even cancelled, driving the Reformist crazy! Is keeping others waiting, the right thing to do?

The spiritual aristocracy of the priesthood functions within an exceptionally simple and effective organisation that respects the linearity of one God, one Church, one clergy and one faithful, and which fosters the parent/child relationships which function so effectively at all levels of Catholicism: structure and organisation are tools which the Church *does* keep simple. Its structure is strongly authoritative and hierarchical, and leaves limited room for outside influence: attempting to apply matrix organisations with their cross-functional combobulation in Romanist 'top-down' structures often meets with confusion and distrust, quite unlike the equanimity with which such forms of organisation are accepted in Reformist societies.

Catholics are encouraged by their clergy to approach God as a community of the faithful rather than as individual believers: such 'collectivism' is linked by an umbilical cord to the fraternal, socialist ethic of Republicanism.[21] In Romanism, man's humanity is expressed through good works to the profit of others, which, unlike the teaching of ascetic Calvinism, *are* held to obtain saving grace and *can* help along the path to salvation.

---

[21] Socio-economic problems can be resolved only with the help of all the forms of solidarity: solidarity of the poor among themselves, between rich and poor, of workers among themselves, between employers and employees in a business, solidarity among nations and peoples. International solidarity is a requirement of the moral order; world peace depends in part upon this.
Catechism of the Catholic Church #1941

The idealistic, flower-loving, Roman Catholic young, rediscovering their spirituality in the 1960's at a time of conflict in Vietnam and of the concomitant peace movement, surfed on Pope John XXIII's wave of renewal of the faith during the Second Vatican Council. The excitement gripped the bishops themselves, working together for three intoxicating years on the new order: the very face of Catholicism was going to change. They had not taken into account that, in 2,000 year of history, the Church has always "been there before,...many, many times!" Tobias Jones in his 'Dark Heart of Italy' sums up very well the inertia that smoothly adapts the Church's rate of change to God's eternity, when he says: *"(Italian church volunteers) would always urge me to read not encyclicals from the Vatican but the liberation theology from the Second Vatican Council (1962-65.) That theology, they said, talked about a social rather than an authoritarian religion and represented the true Church. The Second Vatican Council was an attempt at a modern Magna Carta, an attempt to involve bishops, even the laity, in the decisions of the Church. Many would say that its objectives have by now been entirely defeated by the Church's extraordinary conservatism, but the documents from Vatican II stand out for their lyricism and tolerance."*

Few Roman Catholics have not read the repeated press articles about the seeming conservatism of Pope Benedict XVI. Although he was recognised as a modernist in the seventies during the Second Vatican Council, he later helped to create the conservative review, *Communio*, which has given a more 'traditional' interpretation to the teachings of Vatican II. With those who interpreted Vatican II as a break with the past, Pope Benedict XVI, when he was Cardinal Ratzinger, argued the sense of continuity that characterises the Church. Like his predecessors, he insisted that any change within Catholicism must develop carefully and in line with the experience of previous millennia: twenty centuries of Roman Catholic tradition could not be thrown out just because the world found itself during the Vietnam war at the liberal apex of a long term cycle oscillating between liberalism and conservatism.

Benedict has become Pope in a time of crisis within the Church: the decline of vocations to the priesthood in Europe; the trouble the Church has had with reactionary priests refusing the modern liturgy; the mushrooming of liberation theology in South America; the persecution of Christians in certain Muslim states, all pose a challenge to his skill in guiding this vast structure into its third millennium. Taking a firm grip on the rudder, he appears to have decided to guide the ship of Roman Catholicism 'back to basics.' Three-quarters of all Roman Catholics in 1900 were European: today less the than one-quarter are European. Critical of 'Liberation Theology' that interprets the Gospels as a socio-political enterprise, he pushed, as Cardinal Ratzinger, for a return to religious orthodoxy, tradition and discipline, and for a stop to the continued weakening of Church liturgy: as Pope Benedict, he has reinstated the Latin Mass, kneeling in Church and the priestly practice of placing the host directly on the tongue of the faithful taking Holy Communion: many of these practices would appear to ruffle the "liturgical feathers" of latter day Vatican II supporters.

As much as John Paul II was a 'media star' that the faithful came to watch, Benedict XVI seems to be the theologian that the faithful come to listen to. His first encyclical, *Deus Caritas est*, (God is Love,) set out to clear any misunderstanding in the minds of the faithful between charity (*agape*) and love (*eros*,) and his writing remains theological, hard work and intensely illuminating.

The Church remains attentive to the work of contemporary philosophers: if Plato and Aristotle influenced much of the Catholic theology of the first millennium, the Church closely studies, among others, the work of Kant and of Kierkegaard for their influence on today's ethical thought: philosophical movements provide feedback on the development of contemporary values, and, interpreted in the context of Catholic doctrine, a "weather vane" to guide theologians. Kant's admission that he had found it necessary to deny knowledge in order to make room for faith; Kierkegaard's statement that religious convictions are a matter of faith, not of knowledge, and the work of both in the area of moral philosophy provide an implicit endorsement from highly regarded, recent philosophers for the theology of the Church. Kant took the position that moral worth rests solely upon the quality of the agent's will, and that what really counts is his intention and what he is trying to do. Because this idea seems to interpret morality in a way that overlooks the content of the action, Kant completed his definition through his doctrine of 'practical reason,' adding that the maxim of any action should be that the agent would will it as the universal law: this is the Kantian 'Categorical Imperative,' which has influenced Church thought since Vatican II on the role of conscience in sin. Kierkegaard, in his book, 'Fear and Trembling,' claims that faith possesses a wholly independent status, lying beyond the province of ethical thinking and resisting elucidation in universal or in rational terms.

There can be no doubt of Pope Benedict XVI's erudition; he is working to align the needs of the contemporary Church with its tradition, and appears to use Kantian thought liberally to communicate this vision. He has stated, for example, that faith without reason degenerates into superstition, a remark welcome not only to the ears of the protestant world but also, possibly, to the ears of that part of the South American clergy struggling with superstitious practices. He has worked ecumenically to bring the Church closer to other religions while recognizing and accepting the differences of doctrine, and, in doing so, has positioned the Church on the road to reform without disregarding its tradition.

However, the work of approaching other religions is treacherous. During a theological speech at Regensburg in September 2006, Pope Benedict's remarks, quoted from the reported conversation of a Byzantine emperor in 1391 concerning the spread of faith through violence, seem to have been taken out of context, and inflamed the Islamic world. This speech was intended to be an analysis of what Christianity has taken from Greek philosophy and a discussion of the relation between faith and reason: his point was that faith is not a wall against which reason breaks, but rather an ocean in which reason is lost. Kant had claimed that, "*all attempts to make a purely speculative use of reason in reference to theology are entirely fruitless and, of their inner nature, null and void*:" a remark that shows how much Pope Benedict himself appears to have taken Kant's work seriously, but the event also showed the immense difficulty of his task in protecting the integrity of his Church in a world of increasing religious hostility where Islam is living its 13th century possibly little differently from the way Christendom lived its own. Benedict went on to draw fire from the Jewish world in early 2009 by reintegrating four schismatic bishops to the fold after one had expressed doubts on the extent of atrocities perpetrated against the Jews by the Nazis.

In the realm of achievement, then, the Romanist is led to believe that he ought to be indifferent to the things of this world: if he works, it should be to make ends meet rather than to accumulate capital; true wealth, the New Testament tells him, should be accumulated in Heaven. He therefore holds money to be suspect and of Satan rather than of God. He is discrete about his money because he believes that those around him associate it with evil: he knows he ought not to spend with show, but, when Romanist "machismo" overpowers him, he 'wastes' some on expensive toys, if he can afford them.

The Romanist relationship with mother Church appears to be one of child and parent: the young male hears that it is good to be poor, and, as a man, he tries to convince himself that poverty and weakness are somehow admirable. This struggle to reconcile seemingly contradictory ideas, and the claimed undesirability of money, would lead him to construct a complex, paradoxical worldview to justify such teaching, which does not appear to correspond with human experience and observation: I have called such thought processes 'elliptic,' as opposed to 'linear.' Reinforcing this apparent role of a child, he calls the priest, "Father," a term applied to a man who is neither his natural father, nor in competition with his natural father for his natural mother's affections. In time he discovers this priest's function with respect to *Mother* Church:[22] power seems to lie with her; God's forgiveness seems to lie with him. He defers to the 'spiritual aristocracy' of the priesthood; he associates it with virtue, and he absorbs its mystical teaching to construct his faith. His concept of asceticism is monastic, and, from his youth, he idealises the 'other worldly,' contemplative life as being spiritually superior to his own lay life of earning a living and looking after his family: he may begin to suspect that the true children of God are the clergy.

He unquestioningly accepts dogma on Church authority, having learnt that there is only one truth and that the Church owns it, a church that deploys it through its unchanging laws, procedures and rules for the faithful. Such truths give him confidence in the righteousness of his religion, and the conviction that he will not be damned providing he follows sacramental procedure: he is convinced that Mother Church will be indulgent with him, pick him up and help him, time and again, to wash away the effect of sin. When he is dysfunctional, he believes that because he is constantly pardoned, he can throw cautious virtue to the wind.

Following the guidance of the clergy, Catholics approach God as a community of the faithful rather than as individual believers: Romanist 'collectivism' holds much in common with the republican 'fraternal ethic' (Chapter 5;) both republican citizenship and Romanist communitarianism echo the ideal of protection of the child-like individual by an adult organisation, much as a hen might cluck over her chicks.

The Romanist may believe that heresy is possibly an even greater misdeed than sin, because it leads to *exclusion* from the Church, whereas sin appears to lead to her compassion. Would this idea not echo the exclusion of "heretical" Communist-Party members, as Dubcek was excluded by his old friend, Brezhnev in the 1968

---

[22] The Church...which is called 'that Jerusalem which is above' and 'our mother,' is described as the spotless spouse of the spotless lamb. It is she whom Christ 'loved and for whom he delivered himself up that he might sanctify her.' It is she whom he unites to himself by an unbreakable alliance, and whom he constantly 'nourishes and cherishes.'
Catechism of the Catholic Church #75

Prague Springtime? A belief in collectivism and the fear of heresy might appear to be parallel characteristics of Romanism and of Communism.

A 'dysfunctional child' relationship with religion could stem from associating private virtue with *external* Church spirituality, rather than with the lonely, *internal*, spiritual search of the Calvinist. The *dysfunctional Romanist* may take pardon for granted like a spoilt child, who knows that he can always get away with self indulgence. He may place responsibility for the condition of his soul on the shoulders of the clergy rather than on his own: he may be guilty, but he is never responsible![23] He may believe that, with such divine resources around him, he would never face eternal damnation.

From the earliest days, he learns to use allusion and ellipsis in a way that allows him to communicate the complexity he experiences continuously. He needs detail to buy in; he appreciates form, refinement and elegance of expression. Resigned to the fact that his beliefs do not fit with natural experience, he is nonetheless reconciled with them because he has been taught to place revelation, and not just empiricism, at the highest level:[24] he accepts dogma on faith, and elliptically adjusts his worldview to rationalise seeming paradox.[25]

For the dysfunctional Romanist, nothing is ever pure and simple, and he may believe that only superficial, stupid or naïve people could think it so; for him, complexity leaves room for expediency

---

[23] *Paraphrasing Georgina Dufoix backwards; Member of the Chamber of Deputies and President of the French Red Cross in 1991, she was charged with manslaughter for not having - for budgetary reasons - authorized HIV testing of blood used in transfusions, and claimed on national television that she was,* "responsible, but not guilty."

[24] "I know that I am a prisoner of 2,000 years of the Catholic Church. All Italians are…"
Federico Fellini

[25] The Church's Magisterium exercises the authority it holds from Christ to the fullest extent when it defines dogmas, that is, when it proposes, truths contained in divine Revelation or also when it proposes, in a definitive way, truths having a necessary connection with these, in a form obliging the Christian people to an irrevocable adherence of faith.
Catechism of the Catholic Church #88

and for a consequentialist ethic, where the end can in fact justify the means.

He may not own up to misdemeanour, because only a priest can forgive sin, not ordinary men; willingly losing face in front of others on a pointless question of principle would appear ridiculous at best, and, dangerous, at worst; such "naivety" might even lose him the esteem of his Romanist friends.

He is impatient with those who are more concerned with limiting time rather than with taking it: time is God's gift to man, and insignificant when compared with God's eternity. Time may be money for others, but God's infinite plan has use for neither, so, neither should the Romanist; deadlines are flexible and to be reviewed on the basis of circumstances.

THE ROMANIST IN BRIEF

The Romanist learns that the collective is embodied with more power and authority than the individual himself, and he fears exclusion from it; he learns too that poverty is close to sanctity. His efforts to restrain his natural individualism and to accept ideals of weakness and of poverty promoted through "maternal" power may result in macho reaction, despite the model of reassurance by an authoritative father figure existing within the church collective.

He is unafraid of sin because the procedure of divine forgiveness gives him confidence in his salvation: as a result, he could be dysfunctionally self indulgent, and not always prudent in avoiding occasions of sin: his behaviour seems to integrate a cycle of sin and forgiveness.

Although he personally experiences 'other-worldly' spirituality through the catharsis of divine forgiveness, in the role of a dysfunctional child, he may feel that moral responsibility is not in his own hands but in those of the parental collective of the Church. His ethic may not encompass the need to ask forgiveness of ordinary men, nor to own up to them about his misdemeanours.

He learns to use elliptic thought to reject natural experience in favour of seeming paradox; he compensates the intellectual strain by using Cartesian deductive reasoning. In this respect, his or her thought processes are strongly <u>*synthetic*</u> *and artistic.*

He suffers from a guilt complex about wealth, and considers time to be unimportant.

CHAPTER 3

MONARCHISM

Monarchy in every sense is the Popery of government.
Thomas Paine: Common Sense

For four formative months, starting on 7th October 1502, Niccolò
Machiavelli, a diplomat working for the Florentine republic,
studied the feudal style and work of Cesare Borgia, the son of
Pope Alexander VI: he identified and catalogued a behavioural
model that was not only to influence the lives of monarchs during
and after the Reformation, but also to formalise the tried-and-
tested rules of survival and of the exercise of personal power
considered ever since to be the epitome of monarchical good
sense. During Machiavelli's absence to study the Borgia
household in the Papal state of Romagna on the Adriatic coast, his
home city, Florence, was returned by a new de Medici Pope to its
de Medici overlords, who had ruled it before the creation of the
republic: from the humanistic city Machiavelli had lived in,
Florence changed back into a feudal one.

Feudalism had been conceived as a form of lay aristocracy during
the sixth century, when Pope Gregory the Great separated the
clergy from the laity: it removed the warlike tribal chiefs from
positions of ecclesiastical authority; it simplified their
organisation of warriors and battle, and improved military
management "in a hostile environment."

To curry favour from his returned de Medici masters, Machiavelli
suitably adapted his findings in his essay entitled, 'The Prince:'
its words summarise the tricks of feudalism. Machiavelli's theme
is that the ends of statecraft justify the means; that treachery can

be a most effective tool, and that personal isolation and self reliance are of the essence. He recognises the obsession with power and survival, and advises his prince to behave as a solitary and remote ruler of his feudal subjects. By today's standards, his model is dysfunctional in most respects, but, as the contemporary manual of feudal management, it was indisputably effective, and as today's guide to extreme individualism among Europeans, few can deny its clear sightedness. No doubt is left in the mind of the surprised reader of the tricks 'the Prince' must get up to, to secure his principality.[26]

As an example of what not to do, Machiavelli writes that, during his Italian campaign, the imprudent French King, Louis XII, eliminated the weak while strengthening the powerful; admitted a strong foreign power into his newly conquered territories, and neither lived in, nor attempted to colonise, them. King Louis really did have it all backwards, and Machiavelli goes on to explain why.

This work is a guide, not only to being the Princeling of a city state, but also to being a monarch. Monarchy is dynastic, rooted in its past, and strongly chauvinistic and tribal: it has dominated the constitutional structure of Europe since the sixth century, following the fall of Rome, and, although almost every European country has been a monarchy or a principality at some time or other, this has never been the case in the United States of America except for fleeting, unsuccessful colonial adventures of England and France. It comes as no surprise, then, that monarchical behaviour and attitudes appear both quaint and absurd to Americans. To the monarchist, however, they are far from absurd, because personal gratification and privilege do indeed result from loyal and selfless service to a prince, who is the "fount of all honour."

---

[26] A prince must not worry about a bad reputation for cruelty... The reality of the matter is that princes, who have got their way through bad faith and treachery, have been more successful than those who have always acted loyally.
Niccolò Machiavelli: The Prince

Honour and privilege conferred on an individual by a republic would normally result from merit; however, monarchs have consistently demonstrated ascription of privilege on the basis of birth and kinship. Outside the royal family, ability and talent are just as necessary in serving a feudal prince as a republic, but princes do ascribe privilege on a basis other than that of achievement: in the interests and survival of their families, princes have often brokered a part of their own privilege, offering titles of nobility, land, patronage, and wealth to those who have loyally protected them and to those who think of the interest of their feudal lord: princes, ever watchful, assume the paternalistic mantles of protectors and patrons where it is useful to do so.

Machiavelli advises that bounty must be given only a little at a time so as to last and to be savoured slowly: excessive generosity can damage a prince; it is costly and can displease his subjects because taxation is necessary to finance it. With passing time, a prince is always considered generous anyway, so there is little inconvenience in being avaricious: lack of generosity is a useful vice for the Prince who wishes to survive, and it has the advantage of avoiding an accusation of being a miser if the Prince stops being generous. All the most successful princes have been considered avaricious: to avoid becoming poor and despised, he might as well be rapacious and hateful for a time. It is far wiser for a prince to have the poor reputation of stinginess than to attract hate, as a prince will, if he is to pay for his generosity by plundering the wealth of his subjects.[27]

In post feudal societies, honour is bestowed for military and civil service through titles and dignities which have been established through the ages by royal succession; even the Vatican can be

---

[27] ...the good (*a prince*) does, profits him not, because it is judged as done through necessity and thus unworthy of praise...too much generosity damages the prince, whilst, if he exercises it with moderation, he cannot be accused of avarice, when he must reduce it...a lack of generosity is a useful vice for he who wishes to reign... spending other peoples' money does not reduce, but increases, prestige; it is spending your own that harms you.
Niccolò Machiavelli: The Prince

given to bestowing honours, as its noble orders attest. Military service confers a highly respected social station in monarchies, perpetuating the image of a soldier's *personal* commitment to his monarch, and, as the European constitutional crowns have their palace guards, so the Papacy has its own Swiss Guard. National churches, like the Anglican Church, maintain strong relations with the monarchy, and distinguished service in the clergy carries a status equivalent to that of distinguished service in the military. Individual monarchs appear to feel at ease with their military people and their clergy, who are seen as non-threatening members of their households: for centuries, elder and younger males of noble families have chosen to become soldiers and clerics. On the one hand the monarch assures himself of the personal loyalty of those who will protect him, and on the other, he sustains that special link with religion that justifies his status in the eyes of his subjects as an anointed and, hopefully, pious ruler.

Are the thoughts of Niccolò Machiavelli relevant in today's world of republican egalitarianism? Indeed they are deeply relevant precisely because it is wrong to state that all of Europe is republican and egalitarian. I claim that the remote, formal, class-conscious behaviour of some of the British and of the Scandinavians is the direct consequence of monarchism. Despite the fact that all of these monarchies are now constitutional, I believe that monarchical behaviour itself remains largely unchanged.

A practical example of Machiavelli's guidance appeared in Scotland on 28th November 2004 when the only country in the world to have maintained feudal land law, rooted in the 13th century, abolished it in the interests of crofters and country folk. The Scottish Labour Party was in power, and had defended land reform as one of its first programmes following the country's devolution from the Westminster parliament. The class to have suffered from reform was that of the Scottish feudal barons, men and women whose families had held land of their monarch for centuries as 'feudal superiors,' and who drew income from it as 'feu duties' and fishing rights. Their rights were destroyed at a stroke with, it seems, no compensation voted to them by the Scottish Assembly. The Crown did nothing to intervene to protect their property despite the fact that many of these barons held it through royal charters "for all time" and are the true, ancient aristocracy of Scotland.

Was this lack of royal action to protect its 'own' not foreseeable? Was the Crown not explicitly following Machiavelli's advice given half a millennium previously, when he stated in characteristically aggressive prose, *"The Prince will never be able to defend himself from his subjects, who are so numerous, but he will always be able to defend himself from the nobles, who are in a minority"*? It's hard to meet the desires of the nobles without causing subjects suffering, whereas it's possible to satisfy subjects without causing great suffering overall. The Prince can act against the nobles, but must never be hated by his subjects; a prince supported by the nobles will have greater difficulty than one supported by the people. The stability of monarchy depends on the alliance between the Prince and his subjects; it is hard to assail a prince in a fortress, who is not hated by his people, and it would appear that Charles I and Louis XVI lost their heads because they did not follow the simple rule of putting the subjects first. The aristocracy don't "have it made," at all!

As Machiavelli encourages the young prince to avoid all things that make him hateful or despised, he also advises him to administer unpopular policy through others, because this affords greater safety than trying to rule at first hand; furthermore, greater remoteness leaves him free to react to any circumstance, including sacrificing those who administer his policy.

To keep the aristocracy even further at bay, Machiavelli states that a prince must never rule through barons who could challenge his power and position, and that a parliament is a fine guarantee of a prince's survival because it is a third-party power between the Prince and his subjects, able to subdue a bothersome feudal nobility and to satisfy the people without involving the Prince directly: he can distance himself from the continual conflict that exists between his subjects in submission to the nobility and from potentates, who make themselves unpopular in lifting taxes. Every city has two political movements: a popular one directed against the nobility by subjects who do not wish to be oppressed, and one directed by the nobility who wishes to oppress them. The Ottoman Turks well understood this by refusing altogether to develop an aristocratic caste; they succeeded by ruling for centuries through Janissaries and by taking women of child bearing age from unknown families into the Sultan's harem at the Topkapi in Istanbul.

The risk of the British royal family losing its position to a claim from 'powerful,' raiding barons is anachronistic, and it is no longer the aristocracy's privilege to collect taxes, but does Scottish land reform not represent the spectre of a challenge to monarchy, the thin end of a republican wedge? Such seemingly innocuous measures in the years leading up to 1789 signalled the impending downfall of the French monarchy. As the aristocratic peerage is thrown out of its House of Lords; as the Scottish barons are dispossessed of their property; as members of the royal family are taxed in the same way as the man in the street; as regional interest groups pronounce fashionable statements about republicanism, the British monarchy, if it is not too late, could opt to restore mutual protection with its aristocracy rather than to witness its destruction: such measures taken against Britain's aristocracy may have been unthinkable as recently as 1939. Strong monarchy has always used domination and submission to ensure its survival: Louis XIV brought all the most influential French nobles throughout France to live in the Château of Versailles where he could personally keep an eye on them and maintain them in total dependency; but European constitutional monarchs are no longer in a position to wield such power nor would they need to much longer if the younger generations of British aristocrats consider their birthright as anachronistic as republicans do.

Machiavelli goes to great lengths to train the young prince in the arts of expediency: he considers cruelty to be an appropriate, immediate reaction to a threat to personal safety or to princely assets; cruelty to an individual is justifiable in the collective interest of the people, and therefore is an appropriate tool from time to time. He stresses that men attack through fear or hate, and that those receiving privileges do not necessarily forget previous offences. In the interest of survival, he recommends his Prince to methodically eliminate those who do, or who can, offend him, and never to believe that others will help a prince up should he fall. Men can exact revenge even for small offences, but they can do nothing once they and their families have been destroyed. The quintessence of princely wisdom is to be sensitive to the existence of evil and to know how to recognise it at its source, and the nub of princely pragmatism is simply to be cruel when necessary. Others fear and admire greatness, temperament, strength, and constancy in a prince, but, despite such virtues, he must know how to simulate and to dissimulate. Men are less afraid of attacking a loved prince than a feared one, because their fear of punishment is strong.[28]

Despite the conflict between subjects and aristocrats, Machiavelli nonetheless states that the population has a natural affection for the old nobility: a prince from an ancient monarchical family can benefit from the affection of his people providing that he has not offended them, but the powerful nobles around him always act in their own interest, and one relies on them at one's peril. Machiavelli informs his prince that men are generally ungrateful, talkative, lying, unreliable and avaricious: in time of peace, they are willing to die for the Prince, but in time of danger, nobody steps forward to risk his life. The nobles have always allied themselves with whomever can bring them power: they are not averse to changing prince if they think that the new may be more generous than the old. Those nobles who do not link their fortunes to those of the Prince are either so cowardly as to be exploited or so ambitious as to be dangerous.

---

[28] To monarchize, be fear'd, and kill with looks…
William Shakespeare: King Richard II

Cynicism towards all men, and especially towards the barons, is of the essence. To succeed, a prince must be "part man and part beast:" he must be a fox to recognise treachery, and a lion to fight off the wolves. He must control the nobles' lust for power by blocking the election of those whom he mistrusts: he must sacrifice much to conquer power, but once it has been gained, it is easy to keep, providing he is ready to sacrifice both friends and foes.[29]

The protection of personal power against foreign incursion is a clear vector of princely philosophy.[30] A prince learns early to mistrust foreign countries and to consider all treaties as tenuous: he must never feel confident of his allies, distrusting his frontiers and remembering that, disarmed, he cannot live in peace among armed neighbours? Long periods of peace induce effeminacy and weakness, and the Prince is warned that those who are more dedicated to the pursuit of pleasure, rather than to the preparation for war, lose their power. His military training must lead him to understand that putting off armed attack can only benefit his enemy: in the case of a threat he must act *immediately*; *time is of the essence*; illness becomes incurable if the medicine is given too late.[31]

The advantage of war beyond the spoils of land and property is that it allows the Prince to generously reward his troops and to increase his own prestige by spending other peoples' money. The

---

[29] ...each is ready to die for his prince when the danger of death is far off, but when danger threatens, and the state needs its citizens, no-one is prepared to risk his life...men are generally ungrateful, talkative, lying, vile, mean...men have less fear of a prince who is loved by his people than one who is feared.
Niccolò Machiavelli: The Prince

[30] I know I have the body of a weak and feeble woman, but I have the heart and stomach of a king, and of a king of England too; and think foul scorn that Parma or Spain, or any prince of Europe should dare to invade the borders of my realm.
Queen Elizabeth I speaking to the troops before the Armada; 1588

[31] ... nothing is so fragile or unstable as a reputation for power not supported by its own strength...A prince has no other objective, concern or basic duty than his continual preparation for war. This in fact is the sole prerogative allowed to he who commands.
Niccolò Machiavelli: The Prince

Prince, who is ready for war, can foster the friendship of other princes because, in learning of his power, they will fear to fight him. However, although the Prince is continually encircled by danger, he must be in touch with his own people, because there will always be a foreign enemy ready to help those who have their prince isolated and under siege in his castle: he who is more afraid of his own subjects than of the foreigner should build a castle, but he who fears the foreigner more, should not.

The Prince must also control his subjects through their wealth because men forget the murder of their father more easily than the loss of their riches: those whose property or women have not been touched in the assault on an enemy city live on quietly, because undisturbed landowners who have no motive for revolt live in continual fear of dispossession.[32]

Machiavelli tempers his rhetoric stating that, to protect the personal reputation of a prince, it is generally wiser to be considered merciful than cruel. Men judge more by appearances than by reality itself, so a prince should be *seen* by the people to be virtuous: he should pronounce no word that does not make him appear all indulgence, all loyalty, or integrity, or piety. He is to appear merciful, liberal, and religious, and, if men are to suffer at his hands, it is safer that they should do so only one at a time and in isolation. The Prince should preach charity and loyalty without necessarily practising either, because a man who wishes to remain virtuous among men who are not, will meet sooner or later with disaster; virtue is advisable only insofar as it is *expedient*.

There is no point in keeping one's word if it is not to one's advantage to do so, or if the conditions have changed under which the word was originally given; others will not keep their word unless it is to their benefit, so there is no point in keeping one's

---

[32] ...men should either be treated well or destroyed. This is because they will finally seek revenge for even a minor offence... Violence must be delivered in one blow to leave less of a wound over time, because it lasts but a short while; benefits, however, must be bestowed in small quantities so that they can be fully savoured.
Niccolò Machiavelli: The Prince

own. The Prince should only keep a promise if it is beneficial to do so: he should change his mind with changing circumstances. He must know how to trick and to elude others when it is in the Princely interest.[33]

A reputation for certain vices, but not all, does not necessarily damage his power: expediency is the norm and evil is at times convenient: otherwise how could war be justified? Applying Machiavelli's rules, lying is acceptable; whatever you are accused of, you deny it, you colour it, you minimise it. Whatever it is you have to tell, you don't tell it all. The Prince might think, but never claim that, "my word is *not* my bond," and "my promises are *unlikely* to be kept," or "*only the naive would ever be stupid enough to take what I say at face value.*" Princes, who kept their word, never did as well as those who didn't.[34]

The opportunities for applying Machiavellian principles are legion in business: at the time, for example, of a corporate takeover, all 'professional violence' directed towards the executives of the conquered company must be accomplished fast to destroy resistance and to give the remaining employees time to regain their confidence. Troublesome members of management who are not immediately eliminated later pose a threat in memory of past 'freedom.'[35]

---

[33] A man who wishes to be virtuous among so many who are not, can only expect disaster...there are virtues that lead to ruin and vices that lead to comfort and safety. *Niccolò Machiavelli: The Prince*

[34] Here lies a great and mighty king
Whose promise none relies on;
He never said a foolish thing,
Nor ever did a wise one.
John Wilmot, Earl of Rochester (1647-1680;) Epitaph on Charles II

[35] Whoever determines the power of another will be crushed because his own power is the fruit of either cleverness or strength, and both are held in suspicion by he who becomes powerful...Whoever becomes the lord of a city state used to freedom, and omits to destroy it first, must expect to be destroyed himself; revolution is, in fact, born in the name of freedom... *Niccolò Machiavelli: The Prince*

The Prince should only listen to those whom he has tested and chosen as his ministers, and he should receive advice only as and when he asks for it, and only to make his *own* decisions. You can judge the wisdom of a prince by the quality of the men who surround him: he must know how to recognise talent and to maintain their loyalty.

He is expected to be wise, and cannot tolerate that his decisions be questioned by those who serve him: the idea of teamwork in Machiavellian thought is quite absurd; those who surround the Prince must submit to *his* will alone, 'intuitu personae,' and any minister who steps out of line should instantly be removed.

The Prince must be opportunistic. If two weaker allies are in conflict among themselves, supporting one of the two and helping him to overcome the other always leads to a useful relation of gratitude and dependence. Only an enemy would advise a prince to remain neutral when such an opportunity presents itself: the wise choice is to back the stronger ally and to manoeuvre him into dependence. Conversely, power gained through the will of another is prey to incertitude and to instability: accepting help from a stronger ally leads to the trap of dependence and gratitude.

From antiquity, when Pharaohs resolved their problems by declaring *themselves* gods, monarchy has always espoused the cause of religion in its defence of power and privilege. Religion is an important tool in the hands of a prince, and has been recognised throughout history as most effective support in the exercise of monarchical power. Monarchies have always searched to ally their dynasties with religion: as Machiavelli tells us, "*there has never been an extraordinary legislator who has not had recourse to God, for otherwise his laws would never been accepted.*" Jean-Jacques Rousseau plagiarised him with his own distinctly republican reformulation in 'The Social Contract,' "*...the legislator puts into the mouth of the immortals to compel by divine authority those whom human prudence cannot move...*" Machiavelli admires the Italian ecclesiastical principalities, declaring that they are quite safe as *"they make use of the supernatural and are protected by divine grace."*

The Vatican has always held that ultimate weapon over princes, excommunication. In the Declaration of Arbroath, the noble supporters of King Robert I, the Bruce, an excommunicated Scottish monarch, considered it necessary to appeal in writing to the French Pope, John XXII, to claim their interests against those of the English King, Edward II. The excommunication of Queen Elizabeth I by Pope Pius V from the Roman Catholic Church in 1570 provided the Vatican with the precedent to encourage Philip II of Spain in launching his Armada in 1588, albeit unsuccessfully, against the Britain.[36]

---

[36] FROM POPE PIUS V'S BULL OF EXCOMMUNICATION OF ELIZABETH I
....

2. Prohibiting with a strong hand the use of the true religion, which after its earlier overthrow by Henry VIII (a deserter therefrom) Mary, the lawful queen of famous memory, had with the help of this See restored, she has followed and embraced the errors of the heretics. She has removed the royal Council, composed of the nobility of England, and has filled it with obscure men, being heretics; oppressed the followers of the Catholic faith; instituted false preachers and ministers of impiety; abolished the sacrifice of the mass, prayers, fasts, choice of meats, celibacy, and Catholic ceremonies; and has ordered that books of manifestly heretical content be propounded to the whole realm and that impious rites and institutions after the rule of Calvin, entertained and observed by herself, be also observed by her subjects. She has dared to eject bishops, rectors of churches and other Catholic priests from their churches and benefices, to bestow these and other things ecclesiastical upon heretics, and to determine spiritual causes; has forbidden the prelates, clergy and people to acknowledge the Church of Rome or obey its precepts and canonical sanctions; has forced most of them to come to terms with her wicked laws, to abjure the authority and obedience of the Pope of Rome, and to accept her, on oath, as their only lady in matters temporal and spiritual; has imposed penalties and punishments on those who would not agree to this and has exacted them of those who persevered in the unity of the faith with the aforesaid obedience; has thrown the Catholic prelates and parsons into prison where many, worn out by long languishing and sorrow, have miserably ended their lives. All these matters are manifest and notorious among all the nations; they are so well proven by the weighty witness of many men that there remains no place for excuse, defence or evasion.

3. We, seeing impieties and crimes multiplied one upon another the persecution of the faithful and afflictions of religion daily growing more severe under the guidance and by the activity of the said Elizabeth -and recognising that her mind is so fixed and set that she has not only despised the pious prayers and admonitions with which Catholic princes have tried to cure and convert her but has not even permitted the nuncios sent to her in this matter by this See to cross into England, are compelled by necessity to take up against her the weapons of justice, though we cannot forbear to regret that we should be forced to turn, upon one whose ancestors have so well deserved of the Christian community. Therefore, resting upon the authority of Him whose pleasure it was to place us (though unequal to such a burden) upon this supreme justice-seat, we do out of the fullness of our apostolic power declare the foresaid Elizabeth to be a heretic and favourer of heretics, and her adherents in the matters aforesaid to have incurred the sentence of excommunication and to be cut off from the unity of the body of Christ.

Religion has been an overarching excuse in both instituting and overthrowing monarchies at different times. Henry VIII broke away from Rome to free his hands from Vatican interference in his amorous designs, but he kept the bishops to lead his new Church. His daughter Elizabeth I so recognised the importance of controlling the new faith that she took James Stewart, the son of Mary, Queen of Scots, from his French-reared, Catholic mother, imprisoned her, and brought him up in the new Anglican Church to reign as the future king of a United Kingdom of England and Scotland. The religiously ambivalent Charles I lost his head to a puritanical Oliver Cromwell; the Catholic James II lost his crown to his Calvinist son-in-law, William of Orange; the Stewart pretender, supported by the Catholic French court of Louis XV, was sidelined in 1714 by crowning the protestant Hanoverian prince, George I, the ancestor of current the house of Windsor, who was only 40th in line to the succession through his Stewart mother.

The aristocratic practice of religion in medieval times did not always imply the practice of angelic virtue: a medieval castle just South of Bologna in Italy hides a lovely chapel on the top floor of the keep. In front of the altar a large circular hole in the ground drops some fifteen metres to a dark, festering dungeon below, and, around its lip, covered only by a groundsheet, rigid, sharp, iron blades jut a short way to its centre. When the family invited a chosen enemy to Mass in its chapel, it led its unsuspecting prey to the groundsheet, where he would fall into the trap, and where his body would be lacerated by the blades before falling to certain death, immediate or not.

A prince relies on formality to protect his privacy: at the apex of society, the peerage creates successive class barriers around him and his family, social stratum by social stratum, extending down

---

4. And moreover (we declare) her to be deprived of her pretended title to the aforesaid crown and of all lordship, dignity and privilege whatsoever. Given at St. Peter's at Rome, on 27 April 1570 of the Incarnation; in the fifth year of our pontificate.

through society to construct a graduated, hermetic class structure. In return for their loyalty and discretion, his friends and servants benefit personally from monarchical patronage, privilege, comfort and wealth. Secrecy and confidentiality protect the affairs of the Prince and of his family: information is at a premium because it does not circulate as freely as in egalitarian societies, and individuals are forced to share information through networks. All is done to save face: he must never have to admit error; he must always stand his ground and avoid apology, because admissions and apologies lead to a perception of weakness in a ruler.[37]

Formality in monarchical society is reflected in national behaviour: individuals interact with diplomacy, deference, discretion and tact; people do all they can to appear harmless and to keep their voice down. In such societies, if you smile at an unknown person, he or she may think you're making fun of him or her, or that you're stupid, or that you're a hypocrite, or that you're flirting. At a prince's court, no individual runs the risk of having his prince think this of him.[38] However, low voices and serious faces hurt the egos of tourists, who expect wide, friendly smiles in European streets; monarchists are isolated and class-conscious; they don't smile at those they don't know, so they are considered arrogant, curt, hostile, cold, rude, and offensive: the British trait for irony can possibly be traced back to a sense of withering, unfunny humour so rich in sarcasm, but so carefully neutral in addressing one's prince: however, the combination of the words *irony* and *sarcasm* reveals a third, *contempt*.

In monarchy, hierarchical navigation implies respect of an individual on the basis of where he is in the social pecking order and not of whether his behaviour necessarily commands it.

---

[37] That the King can do no wrong is a necessary and fundamental principle of the English constitution.
Sir William Blackstone, 1723-1780: Commentaries on the Laws of England

[38] I'm afraid you've got a bad egg, Mr. Jones
Oh no, my Lord, I assure you! Parts of it are excellent!
Punch, Vol CIX p222, 1895

Respect of social hierarchy is drilled into the infant from the earliest age: he is taught politeness and manners which typify the finely balanced rules of communication established to protect the self esteem of the middle classes on the social ladder: manners provide suitable deference to one's superiors; they comfort the subjection of the vassal to his feudal lord, and protect the disinterest of the superior in his social inferior.[39] In monarchical societies, individuals avoid using first names on first introduction and generally avoid informality because casual communication intimidates feudal superiors. The approach is quite different from the big grin and the, *"Just call me Bob!"* which seems *de rigueur* in other countries.

The French lead the world in formality with the 'baise-main' lady's hand kissing, which is a habit particular to males of the old aristocracy, or who would have liked to be. In common with upper class Italians, Germans, and Spaniards, they use the formal version of the second person singular, which is quite absent from the English language since the disappearance of "thee" and "thy," in addressing people they don't know well; it is a useful tool for establishing class distance at the outset. Despite the fact that France has been a republic on and off since the late 19th century, the manners of the French remain monarchical, and their form of politeness, remote and sober. The Republic has at least established the egalitarian habit now of using "*Monsieur*" rather than "*Garçon*" for calling a waiter in a restaurant, and there is a growing tendency among the youth, as always, to loosen the conventions of what is and what is not polite. However, the educated French continue to charm with their show of resistance at being first through a door, and invariably say "*Monsieur*" or "*Madame*" at the end of any phrase addressed to an unknown person. This code of politeness appears less obsequious than the American habit, or indeed of the French one, of placing that "*Sir*,"

---

[39] The strongest man is never strong enough to be master all the time, unless he transforms force into right and obedience into duty. ...feudal government, an irrational system if ever there was one, and contrary both to natural justice and to all sound polity.
Jean-Jacques Rousseau: The Social Contract

which grinds so on the British ear at the end of a phrase: the Brits judge it to be self abasing; they would never dream of using "*Sir*" unless speaking to an obvious superior such as a senior officer, a diplomat or a member of the royal family.

In France it is the height of bad manners to stop somebody in a street to ask directions without starting with the words, "*Excuse me, 'Monsieur,' for disturbing you, but can you help me...*" The broad grin from a tourist on the street with that, "*Hey, buddy, can you tell me where....*" leads the Frenchman to cringe, scowl and to crawl into an unfriendly shell. France was a monarchy until not so long ago, and French manners are formal: the informal foreigner in the street would do well to be similarly discreet.

The maintenance of power within a monarch's family respects an ideal of the protection of individual rights, inheritance and family property, and not of state rights. In monarchies it is perfectly acceptable to be born rich, and such societies defend private property and inherited privilege, leading the nobility to quickly close its ranks and to exclude those who threaten them: conversely, they are left clannishly open to those servants and ministers, who protect their estates. The recent experience of the Scottish barons would show that the British monarchy appears to give perhaps less weight today to values which are germane to the protection noble assets; but, in general, individual wealth, whether earned, given or inherited, is perfectly acceptable and has usually been protected from the predatory and avaricious state: there is little of that egalitarian drive implicit in the republican model that seemingly authorises a proletariat to fleece its aristocracy.

Jean-Jacques Rousseau's phrase, "*the strongest is never strong enough to stay in control unless he transforms strength into right and obedience into duty,*" illustrates the thrust from feudal, to constitutional, monarchy. The Magna Carta, one of the first great exercises in constitutional monarchy, was imposed by the nobles on King John much to his discomfort. King John looked upon the written word as a bothersome constraint, and signed the document against his will; putting decisions in writing limited the options he had to go back on his word, and, to this day, the United Kingdom still has no written constitution: however, the creation of constitutional monarchy has guaranteed the survival of the royals who have followed King John to the British throne for the past 800 years.

It is said that Henri III of France had a copy of 'The Prince' with him when he was assassinated in 1589. We may not endorse all that Machiavelli wrote, yet, it's 'tough at the top,' and, as a form of leadership in a war-torn world, his guidance is summed up in the wisdom of Jean de la Fontaine (1621-1695,) when he said, "The cause of the strongest is always the best."[40]

By way of summary, Machiavellian monarchism exposes a model of dysfunctional individualism.

Highest honour comes from service to individuals with aristocratic status, and privilege is expected in return for the devotion of the one who serves; however, as the aristocrat knows he can rely on no-one but himself if he falls, then he who serves must never expect to enter into the aristocrat's confidence. Men can always be relied upon to act in their own interest; thus, a cynical understanding of behaviour, mistrust, and circumspection are all key to survival, because the servant may well side with another master. In his own interest and in that of his immediate family, the master remains isolated and xenophobic.

The ideal of individual feudal submission results from willing attachment to an acknowledged superior that leaves no room for collective submission, nor for 'teamwork,' which is a purely republican, and possibly Romanist, tool: monarchical relations are structured around individuals across class barriers, and not around the 'collective.' Interest outside self interest is without meaning, and the republican, fraternal ideal of coming second to the collective is quite anathema to monarchical principles.

---

[40] "La raison du plus fort est toujours la meilleure."

The interpersonal distance created between the master and the servant manifest in formality of speech and manners leads both to adopt codes of conduct, forms of politeness and discretion designed to protect one from the other. Rights and duties are idealised to lock in the subservient behaviour the master requires of his servant.

Complex social stratification is created using class barriers, every individual finding himself isolated within his own class. Classes quickly close their ranks to the dangerous, to the non-conforming and to the excluded, provoking keen sensitivity to social inclusion and exclusion. The sense of hierarchy is pervasive in monarchy; it naturally separates those who are different, and allows the rich to flaunt their wealth safely within their own class.[41] The class structure leads to increasing levels of privilege through the class system, and, with privilege, come riches.[42]

The master uses patronage to guarantee his survival and the longevity of his family; much as the Prince, who is the fount of all honour, confers honour to nourish loyalty: society benefits from the knock on effect, where the servant can expect his own assets to be as much protected from pilfering government as the Prince protects his own.

The need to protect the 'face' of the superior is of paramount importance too. The master is careful to be seen to be virtuous, never finding himself in a position to need to apologise, nor to admit error, and his immediate entourage is expected to work to

---

[41] ...the English are class-obsessed...The Duchess of Devonshire treasures the baffled comment written in the visitors' book at Chatsworth, their pile in Derbyshire: 'Saw the Duke in the garden. He looked quite normal."
Jeremy Paxman: The English

[42] The upper classes may have lost their political power, but they still manage to set the social tone and determine the aspirations of the ambitious. So, when the successful businessman makes his first £10 million, he starts scanning the pages of *Country Life* for a manor house to buy.
Jeremy Paxman: The English

project his image of loftiness and of graciousness. The monarchist's behaviour supports an image of virtue: he is formal, tactful, diplomatic, discrete and aloof with those below, and deferent and subservient when dealing with those above: he speaks in a quiet voice to reinforce his appearance of harmlessness to a superior, but he may well 'bray' like a donkey at an inferior to assert his status. He claims his right to change his mind, and his decisions are more guided by expediency than by rigid principle, which so often causes needless harm. Servants must never expect promises, because they cannot expect the master to keep them unless it is perfectly convenient to do so, and this is often not the case.

Confidentiality and family safety imply the control of information, which is delivered and received through private networks: there is no ideal of freedom of information, nor, indeed, of the need to circulate it beyond those who need to know. Confidentiality protects the affairs of the master, and information is not intended to descend the social ladder; however, information ascending the social ladder provides the servant with a measure of power across the class barrier; he may or may not elect to barter what he knows.

Isolation protects the master from being over generous, or from being perceived as avaricious; and, as the number of class barriers increases, the more remote he becomes, and the less he can be judged by his inferiors.

THE MONARCHIST IN BRIEF

Dysfunctional monarchical behaviour centres on the feudal inviolability of personal property, on its protection from the fingers of the 'pilfering' collective and on the protection of the right to inheritance. The individual comes before the collective and there is no concept of submission to the collective good. This leaves little room for the idea of teamwork; the Monarchist's values are strongly <u>individualistic</u>.

Society classes itself into layers of privilege: members of a class isolate themselves from those of other classes heightening sensitivity to hierarchy, exclusion and status.

The idealisation of rights and duties makes it advisable to serve an individual from a higher class who has the status and power to confer privilege and to provide patronage. Strict codes dictate behaviour across class barriers, and communications are facilitated by formality of speech and of manner.

The master is expected to appear lofty, gracious, formal, tactful, diplomatic, discrete, aloof, and never to apologise nor to admit error to those below him. He expects all to act in their own interest, including those who serve him, and so he mistrusts all around him: he relies on himself and on no-one else; he volunteers information on a need-to-know basis and claims the right to change his mind and not to keep promises. He has no scruples about expediency when the survival of his lifestyle is at stake. He remains isolated and nurtures a xenophobic suspicion of his neighbours.

The servant will act like his master towards those of inferior classes, but to his master, he is careful to appear deferent and subservient. He knows that society will never allow him across the class barrier and that, as a result, he cannot expect to enter into the confidence of his master. He is careful to speak with a quiet voice to reinforce his appearance of harmlessness: he remains confidential and discrete, and relies on his private information network to find out what is going on.

CHAPTER 4

REFORMISM

...the religious forces which express themselves through (ascetic Protestantism) are the decisive influences in the formation of national character.
Max Weber: *The Protestant Ethic and the Spirit of Capitalism*

In his book, "The English," Jeremy Paxman describes recent developments in the Anglican Church: he paints the picture of a Church that shuns dogmatism and that searches to provide its faithful with space and freedom. Anglicanism presents a spectrum of religious practice extending from Methodism and Evangelicalism to traditional Anglo-Catholicism, whose theology remains but one step from traditional Roman Catholic teaching: one of our good friends is a Welsh priest, who, after 20 years of Anglican priesthood, applied to the Roman Catholic bishop of his diocese to become a Catholic priest: he was ordained without further ado, and is now successfully running a delightful parish in the South of France, hearing confessions and singing the Latin mass in his rich, Welsh tenor voice as though he had spent his whole youth in a Roman Catholic seminary. As soon as the Church of England faces resistance in its ranks, it regularly appears to get threats from its priests to defect to Rome.

Jeremy Paxman claims that Anglicanism has always owed more to Erasmus than to Luther, and that it appears to be more firmly rooted in our everyday world than in the next. He states that the Church of England has found a formula that meets the needs of English religion; he calls it pragmatic, comfortable and unobtrusive. The achievement of Anglicanism has been to tame a deep seated suspicion of clericalism, and to be so adaptable as to encompass all sorts of movements. The former Archbishop of Canterbury, Dr Robert Runcie, is quoted as having said, *"There are other churches in Christendom which take pride in their lack of ambiguity in doctrine or leadership, or in monolithic interpretation of the gospel. Anglicanism, by contrast, is a synthesis, and a synthesis necessarily unites thesis and antithesis."*

Paxman reminds his reader of an ancient nationalist image of Protestantism: when Catholic France and Spain were united against Britain during the Reformation it seemed *impossible to be both a Roman Catholic and a British patriot*: John Foxe's Book of Martyrs was exposed in every Anglican church, graphically describing the persecution of protestants by 'Bloody' Mary Tudor. Nationalism is also on display in the Reformed Churches, such as the Scots Presbyterian churches, where the St Andrew's cross, or Saltire, is often exhibited, much as the cross of St. George is at times on show in Anglican churches. Rare indeed are such manifestations of nationalism seen in Catholic churches: Catholicism has been more an object of hostile separation from states; from the French state in 1905; during the Mexican Revolution; in the Spanish Constitution of 1931; and leading up to the Lateran Accords in Italy in 1929, which were possibly less painful, but nonetheless traumatic.

Machiavelli encouraged his Prince to use religion in support of his crown: the British monarchy has done this well down through the centuries, exploiting the title, 'Defender of the Faith,' originally bestowed upon the younger Henry VIII by a grateful Pope Leo X, but rescinded by Pope Paul III. This title, retained by an act of parliament to allow Henry VIII to continue using it, will be assumed by Prince Charles when he inherits the Crown: the remark he is reputed to have made, "I hope to be the defender of *faiths,*" would illustrate the reasonableness of Anglicanism in the increasing cultural complexity of the land over which, no doubt, he will one day reign; but was his remark intended to defend Islam, Hinduism and Judaism as much as Christianity? What has

become of the fiery Christian kerygma that led a Pope to attribute
the title to his ancestor in the first place?

Nearly 70 million Christians belong to Lutheran churches
worldwide, and many of these reside throughout Northern
Europe, including Germany and Scandinavia. This elder branch of
protestant Christianity directly embodies Martin Luther's teaching
consequent upon the Protestant Reformation. Lutheranism is
distinct from the teaching of the Reformed churches, which are of
more Calvinist influence: Luther was not totally opposed to
certain sacramental and liturgical practices, and taught a more
optimistic approach than the doctrine of predestination in
supporting a doctrine of justification by faith alone.

In the background of the Reformation, Martin Luther in Germany,
and Huldrych Zwingli, Jean Calvin and John Knox in
Switzerland, in France, in the Low Countries and in Scotland,
worked to promote Protestantism and drove a heavy doctrinal
wedge between Rome and much of Northern Europe. The
Reformation caused the cultural trauma following the
Renaissance which was to transform Europe from a medieval,
feudal-Roman society into one that integrated the new collective,
lay values that would prepare the Age of Enlightenment.

European politics had been controlled up to then by a network of
monarchies, dominated since the 9th century in central Europe by
the Holy Roman Empire,[43] and which held a wide spectrum of
relations with Rome, some very friendly, some very tense. The
new teaching forced a religious realignment of many of the
Northern princes and monarchs, such as Frederick IV, the Elector
Palatine, and Henry VIII, and led to destructive wars of religion
throughout Europe. The St Bartholomew's Day massacre in
France in 1572, when the monarchy engineered the extermination
of a swath of the Huguenot nobility, led to the first flight of
influential Protestants from French soil: no doubt the French

---

[43] Although Charlemagne had been crowned Emperor by the Pope on Christmas day 800 at
Aachen, the first to be effectively recognised as Holy Roman Emperor was Otto I the Great,
Duke of Saxony, King of Germany, King of Italy, in 962.

Regent, Catherine de Medici was irritated at the imprisoning by Queen Elizabeth I of Mary, Queen of Scots, the daughter of Mary of Guise, who had been her contemporary at the French court. Catherine reacted more strongly against the French Protestants than she should have done, but, as a Florentine, it was to be expected that she would apply Machiavellian solutions to her problems. The House of Orange was called upon, and subsequently, the House of Hanover, to put an end to the reign of the Catholic Stewarts in Britain. As recently as 1701, the Act of Settlement confirmed England as a protestant state and prevented Catholics from ascending the throne or from marrying into the Royal Family: in 2009, this act, perhaps anachronistically, is still on the Statute Book, but Prime Minister Gordon Brown, is talking of repealing it.

Of the forms which Protestantism took following the Reformation, ascetic Calvinism chose the road farthest from that of Roman Catholicism, which had guided European metaphysical thought for more than a millennium before the upheaval.[44] Jean Calvin, in his development of Martin Luther's lead, strongly opposed Roman mysticism, and chose the Bible and worldly knowledge as the lenses through which to focus upon man's relationship with God and his own salvation. With 'iron logic,' he demonstrated that man is predestined either to eternal salvation or to eternal damnation and that he is in no position to modify that destiny, nor are sacraments or good works of use in shifting him any closer to salvation.[45]

---

[44] And Catholicism has to the present day looked upon Calvinism as its real opponent...the complete elimination of salvation through the Church and the sacraments...was what formed the absolutely decisive difference from Catholicism.
Max Weber: The Protestant Ethic and the Spirit of Capitalism

[45] With Calvin the 'decretum horribile' (*i.e. the doctrine of predestination*) is derived not, as with Luther, from religious experience, but from the logical necessity of his thought; therefore its importance increases with every increase in the logical consistency of that religious thought...By founding its ethic in the doctrine of predestination, (Calvinism) substituted for the spiritual aristocracy of monks outside of and above the world the spiritual aristocracy of the predestined saints of God within the world.
Max Weber: The Protestant Ethic and the Spirit of Capitalism

The Calvinist approach to sin is quite different from that of the Catholic: because each person is predestined either for salvation or for damnation, saving grace cannot be accumulated through worldly virtue or good works, and it cannot be conferred through repentance, in the presence of a priest, or not. As God is all powerful and all knowing for all time and because man can only be either saved or damned, God has predestined each man and woman for either damnation or salvation. Calvinist doctrine claims that man is "doomed to an inexorable fate admitting of no redress:" the Fall has left him "dead in sin,"' and he is in no position to save himself: he is entirely in God's hands and can do nothing but submit to his destiny of which God is aware from all eternity: *"some men and angels are predestined unto everlasting life, whereas others are ordained unto everlasting death."* This is the logical consistency of Calvinism rooted only in this worldly thought and in the words of the Bible. Calvin considered that the alternative hypothesis of free will and of salvation through good works was rooted in construction rather than in revelation. The sinner faces his Creator alone: he is, in fact, so alone that other protestant creeds have tended to drift away from the strict doctrine of predestination.[46] Luther, for example, took an altogether softer view, and accepted, for example, that humility and simplicity could help pave the way to salvation.

Such a dire worldview engenders concern and, according to Max Weber, sullenness among the faithful, especially as good works are useless in attaining salvation, even though they are necessary to increase God's glory in this world. The behaviour expected from a Calvinist, for which John Knox was famous when he established the Presbyterian Church in Scotland, is serious, unsmiling and uncompromising with sin; the boyish or girlish

---

[46] The religious believer can make himself sure of his state of grace either in that he feels himself to be the vessel of the Holy Spirit or the tool of the divine will. In the former case, his religious life tends to mysticism and emotionalism, in the latter to ascetic action;...Calvin viewed all pure feelings and emotions, no matter how exalted they might seem to be, with suspicion... The radical elimination of magic from the world allowed no other psychological course than the practice of worldly asceticism.
Max Weber: The Protestant Ethic and the Spirit of Capitalism

grin is held to be in contradiction with Calvinist behaviour, which must be sober at all times. As a result, the stereotypical ascetic Reformist appears to express a limited range of emotions, leading his life of lonely virtue without passion, where self control is paramount to proving to himself that God has elected him to salvation from all eternity.[47]

Max Weber wrote that the Methodist claims a *"pure feeling of absolute certainty of forgiveness and the undeserved possession of divine grace,"* and that the Quakers, in their silent vigil and repose, *"wait for the Spirit to descend and claim rebirth through individual revelation."* Both of these claims show a hint of mystical catharsis, much as that afforded by the Catholic sacraments. However, Calvinism refuses such mysticism and accepts only the authority of the Bible as the normative guide: it rejects the vast swath of non-biblically based tradition of the Church fathers; the insistence of the Reformers on returning to authoritative, biblical texts, rather than giving credence to tradition, led, within Protestantism, to its general distrust of mysticism and of elaborate interpretation: Calvin's doctrines are hence reputed to be linear and logically consistent. He mistrusted 'ornate' content in the liturgy and 'emotional' content in theology, and was quick to deride it as superstition: religious emotion distracts rational thought, and the absence of passion in the sight of God is a far more appropriate attitude to have than one of the numinous if the faithful are to cool headedly judge where lies the road of virtue. The Calvinist holds that most of the doctrinal claims concerning the sacraments are *"illusion;"* in this world, the mystical must submit to the rational.

In Calvin's 'this worldly' tradition, the Protestant Ethic is identified with that pragmatism and simplicity which can be

---

[47] There once was a man who said, Damn!
It is borne in upon me I am
an engine that moves
in predestinate grooves,
I'm not even a bus I'm a tram.
Maurice Evan Hare, 1889-1967

couched in clear and concise language. In reformist societies, "no" is intended to mean *no*, and language is intended to be explicit, direct, clear and 'linear.' To convince within reformist societies you must first make sense.[48] The pragmatism of the protestant Henri IV of France in accepting the crown of France providing he became a Catholic is typified in his remark (ca. 1593) that, "Paris is surely worth a Mass."[49] The *"linearity"* of Protestantism can be described as a form of *"this-worldly"* thought strongly supporting ideals of theological simplicity and of clear, concise and explicit language. Talk and the written word must communicate fact, and mystical terms are held to be without meaning. The insistence in this world, on pragmatism and on human experience favours empirical and inductive thought, which is the approach validated shortly before the Reformation by the rediscovery of Aristotle's thinking on the scientific method: according to this philosopher, arguments, abstract or otherwise, could only validly be substantiated by evidence and, to be acceptable, theory had to resist factual observation.

A pious Calvinist does well to consider himself *chosen* if he is to have any self confidence at all, and he is only likely to do so if he perceives success in his *'calling:'* lack of confidence in one's salvation is dispiriting, and there is no intermediary in Calvinism able to place the faithful back on the road to salvation as a Catholic priest might do through the sacraments. Those 'elect,' who are predestined for salvation, are conscious of God working through them and of their good works being a sufficient sign of salvation, and not, as in other creeds, a way to win it. Confidence in one's virtue and salvation leads to the idea of a 'spiritual aristocracy' of 'worldly saints,' and to a strong distaste for sin and conceivably for those who commit it. Does this certainty of virtue

---

[48] Orthodox! Orthodox!-
Wha believe in John Knox-
Let me sound an alarm to your conscience:
A heretic blast
Has been blawn in the Wast,
That what is not sense must be nonsense
Robert Burns; The Kirk's Alarm
[49] "Paris vaut bien une messe!"

and suspicion of sinners not leave the *dysfunctional Reformist* open to a hint of arrogance and intolerance, not to say of bigotry?[50] Is there not a risk of intolerance jumping into overdrive when inflamed by the morally absolutist ideal of the 'right thing to do?'

Intolerance could well appear on the dysfunctional face of Reformism, but is in no way limited to it alone. The behaviour of John Knox in Edinburgh from 1559 is an example of the morally absolutist approach to what is good and right:[51] such was his confidence in his 'universal' ethic, that he went about setting his Queen, the Catholic, French-speaking Mary, Queen of Scots with single minded efficiency on the long road to her final execution. Arguably, Mary had been just as bigoted in persecuting John Knox some years before, and her own Church had hardly been a model of 'tender, loving kindness' during the Inquisition.

Reformist societies share universal beliefs, such as 'honesty being the best policy;' they glorify punctuality, frugality, industry, credit worthiness, simplicity, labour, discipline, in fact all of the utilitarian facets of virtue. The Reformist values temperance, reliability, duty and hard work, and views any resort to expediency as a sign of damnation. The behaviour of the "honourable" Victorian schoolboy may well stem from such a universal ethic: he owns up to his misdeed in front of all the class on a point of principle; because he has been led to believe that it is the 'right thing to do.' He grows up to believe that 'his word is his bond' and, despite the debunking of this idea by Machiavelli, that rigid adhesion to 'principle will always win through in the end.' It is the admirable ideal that allows drivers in the American Mid-West to draw up at a four-way city crossing without traffic

---

[50] This consciousness of divine grace of the elect and holy was accompanied by an attitude towards the sin of one's neighbour, not of sympathetic understanding based on consciousness of one's own weakness, but of hatred and contempt for him as an enemy of God bearing the signs of eternal damnation. *Max Weber: The Protestant Ethic and the Spirit of Capitalism*

[51] The grosser pagans contented themselves with divinising lust, incest and adultery; but the predestinarian doctors have divinised cruelty, wrath, fury, vengeance and all the blackest vices. *David Hume: Essays Moral, Political and Literary*

lights and to cross over, each in turn, without ending up in a three hour gridlock, which is what happened to me in Paris on one occasion when traffic lights went down. Such an ethic implies volunteering the truth, the whole truth, and nothing but the truth, *even if it kills you*, and the conviction that ultimate responsibility is, in all cases, lonely and individual.

Barack Obama went on television in February 2009 to say that *he* had "screwed up" in the nomination of a new secretary to his Cabinet, who had been criticised for tax avoidance; the fact was that the President was *not* the one who had committed the malfeasance; and would he have made the nomination had he known this would happen? Nonetheless, *he* took some blame; others may read that he was taking some responsibility. Be that as it may, my question is whether or not doing so was likely to endear him to the nation?

Assuming that a person is not guilty, is it perceived to be a sign of virtue to own up to something he or she has not done? I met an American industrial manager who spent his time during meetings with his subordinates repeatedly apologising for things he had not done and even for things he intended to do, irritating some of the Europeans reporting to him. Such behaviour can come as a surprise both to Romanists, who only own up to God through priests, and to Monarchists, who would expect people of stature never to own up to anything at all: they would probably class such behaviour as dysfunctionally Reformist, and, in the case of the Monarchist, conceivably even as a sign of weakness.

Military intervention by the West and its allies in Muslim states illustrates, in my view, a similar problem with this ethic; what appears as a form of "angelic'" conviction of leadership in an exclusive understanding of the 'the right thing to do' leads, I believe, so often to *doing the wrong thing*, at least from the point of view of 'invaded' Muslims, who may just so happen to disagree with the approach. I am absolutely not agnostic, but when protestant fathers of the United States proclaimed to the world that "*in God we Trust*" on their currency, did they not ask whether this national proclamation disturbed agnostics, atheists, anti-clericals, or individuals who may have conceived their gods differently from theirs? In the admirable 1994 Twentieth Century Fox remake of "Miracle on 34th Street," a New York judge uses that proclamation, which is written on the 1 dollar note, to rule that, if the American government can overwrite its currency with such a statement, which is based on trust, then the City of New York can equally affirm its trust in the existence of Santa Claus.

Protestants and Catholics in the streets of Belfast have suffered from years of mutual intolerance, with, no doubt, both factions capable of dysfunction. Belief in knowledge and ownership of a morally absolutist ethic lies behind the iron inflexibility and misunderstanding of intolerance: for example, centuries before the tragedy of Belfast, was it not bigotry that justified feudal crusaders returning from the Holy Land burning on July 22 1209 an estimated 20,000 defenceless men, women and children, in their Southern French city of Béziers for harbouring heretic Cathars? That event turned a large part of that region of France against the Vatican and against the French Crown for centuries to come, and laid a solid foundation for French Protestantism in the Navarre region. When the crusading commander, Arnaud d'Amaury, was asked during the siege how he would distinguish the Cathars from the Catholics, he is reputed to have said, *"Burn them all: God will recognise his own."*

The ascetic Reformist is upset by vice, particularly among those whom he has elevated to positions of power over society. An American politician caught lying is severely reprimanded and can be impeached, whereas in Romanist society, a politician almost might be *expected* to 'bend' the truth; in fact, if he didn't, those who put him in power might consider him naïve and unqualified for such responsibility. In one of the first series of the monumental Fox television production, '24,' thousands of Europeans, South American, Middle-Easterner and Oriental viewers probably despaired of ever coming to terms with the concept of the 'right thing to do' as they speechlessly watched an actor impersonating Senator David Palmer, a black Democrat presidential nominee, turn his teenage son over to the police when he didn't have to, and repudiate his wife of 20 years for having supported him with "excessive" ambition, all on the grounds that it was the 'right thing to do.'

It is not difficult to understand why so many would find much to admire in the principle that such behaviour is intended to portray: indeed, many American voters appear to have admitted that their support of Barack Obama during the 2008 Presidential election had been influenced to some extent by the virtuous image of a black president portrayed in the role of David Palmer; admiration of such behaviour appears to be pervasive in American society. However, Mr. Obama's own comments on his Whistle-Stop voyage to the White House were, in my view, absolutely correct and pertinent in his attack on his nation's "small thinking, prejudice and bigotry;" there must indeed be "better angels."[52]

Of course it is wrong to criticise men of virtue; I am simply claiming that potentially destructive action taken on the sole basis of *principle* is in my view downright dangerous; the oversimplification of the so called 'right thing to do' is a component of *dysfunctional Reformism*. If politics is the "art of the possible," does it not rather require pragmatism? Would I be the only one to find oversimplification in those who run the politics of a country, distressing? Are seemingly angelic men, who are portrayed on TV as having made little progress since they learnt their virtue in the nursery, really believed by TV viewers as qualified to protect their country against a nuclear strike or to handle international diplomatic crises? Would such caricatures really think twice before launching a nuclear war on a question of '*principle*?'

---

[52] "What is required is a new declaration of independence, not just in our nation, but in our own lives - from ideology and small thinking, prejudice and bigotry - an appeal not to our easy instincts but to our better angels."
Barack Obama, January 17th 2009 (as reported in the Arab Times of Kuwait, January 18th 2009 at the start of his Whistle Stop tour to the White House from Philadelphia's 30th St. Station.)

In the 1999 Cohen bros film, "The Big Lebowski," Walter, the Duke's friend, who boasts his devotion to the Jewish Sabbath, but who is really a Polish Catholic, claims, to a background of Mozart's 'Requiem,' that, *"doing the right thing, whatever the cost, makes the man."* For a dysfunctional Romanist, the thrust of Walter's statement sounds rather more like *dysfunctional Reformism.* With their characteristically sharp observation of middle class America, the Cohen brothers' films penetrate the very heart of its society: neither the Duke nor Walter is an intellectual, both are work-shy rednecks; their behaviour seems to ape this penetration by TV-soap moral absolutism of the very roots of American values.

I agree that a politician must be a good man, but I don't believe that he should be naïve too, and neither did Machiavelli, who knew more than most about the art of politics. Yet, perhaps such a model *is* Machiavellian: if the image of public virtue admired by a nation is indeed morally absolutist, then, because the Prince must be *seen to be* virtuous, his *public image* probably ought to be morally absolutist too. However, had God intended us to see the world in black and white, he would not have given us colours and shades of grey; so I frankly prefer to think that Reformist politicians, like everyone else's politicians, ought to be "part man and part beast;" a fox to recognise treachery, and a lion to fight off the wolves. The problem is that lesser men and women may believe in the angelic image and go on to apply moral absolutism in their own fields with not always a fortunate outcome.

Were Romanism and Machiavelli's Prince left behind in the 'Old World' when the Mayflower set sail? Maybe; maybe not, yet the morally absolutist, angelic image appears to me to stand out as a dysfunctionally Reformist, American caricature.

In 1904, Max Weber published *'The Protestant Ethic and the Spirit of Capitalism,'* claiming that Capitalism finds its roots in ascetic Calvinism. His essay draws on the practice of late 19th century Calvinism in Germany and describes the rationale for the accumulation of wealth through pious work and ascetic self denial; it also discusses certain doctrinal differences between the principal German protestant movements, including Pietism, which combined Lutheranism with certain ideas of the Reformed churches. Some have criticised his work, claiming, for example, that the Catholic Italian city states, such as Venice or Genoa, during the Middle Ages were already hotbeds of trade and money, and thus of Capitalism, at a time predating the work of Calvin. Be that as it may, Weber's work has a wide following among sociologists, and, though certain points can certainly be disputed, there is consensus concerning his ideas, particularly as the birth of Capitalism in the United States does appear to be strongly linked to the 'Mayflower' tradition of the puritan founding fathers, which characterises the 'waspish' ethic of the Eastern seaboard. In 1926, a lecturer at the London School of Economics, R.H. Tawney, published his influential 'Religion and the Rise of Capitalism,' bringing considerable impetus and credibility to the Weber Thesis.

Calvin stated that worldly activity rather than mysticism serves to increase the glory of God, and that it is morally correct to fulfil one's duty in worldly affairs. Monasticism was seen by him to be a selfish withdrawal from worldly obligations because the true calling implies work for the benefit of God's *rational* universe; attempting to flee worldly morality through monastic asceticism is not as pious as fulfilling one's worldly obligations with virtue; duty in worldly affairs is the highest form of morality accessible to mankind. However, the personal discipline of the 'worldly saints' favours a rigid ethical framework which is in some ways nonetheless comparable with the type that ascetic Catholicism induces in members of its clergy.

If labour and frugality merit wealth as God's earthly gift, then it is proper that wealth should be used to increase His glory. The Calvinist labours conscientiously for this and finds wealth a sign of His approval: if he leads a sober and industrious career crowned with achievement, he has probably been 'called' to be

one of God's 'elect,' that is to say he is predestined for salvation.[53]
If God has shown one of his elect a chance of profit then he must
take it, otherwise he refuses the stewardship of the good things
which God has granted him. The practice of Calvinism thus
justifies business acumen and financial achievement providing
wealth is accumulated with practical piety and with confident,
hard labour pleasing to God; this constitutes the 'this-worldly,'
capitalist ethic of Calvinism. However, the frugality of
asceticism, which is the corollary of Calvinist wealth, leads also
to a caricature of avarice and to possibly an immoderate
abhorrence of worldly pleasures.

Within the lonely certitude of predestination, success in business
is a sign of salvation, and, because a man is expected to be an
obedient steward of God's gifts, he must hold them undiminished
and respond to his calling to develop them: wealth is the virtuous
outcome of his performance of duty and of his reply to his calling;
God blesses the trade of the sober man of business; accumulating
capital is a sign of virtue.

If the dysfunctional Reformist does not impose mortification on
the man of wealth, he may however be tempted to abase the
beggar: the corollary of finding virtue in wealth is to find disgrace
in poverty, not because of the suffering it provokes but because
the beggar's plight implies that he is not among the worldly
saints, otherwise God would have smiled on his labour:[54] absent
from the elect, the beggar is marked with his dark destiny; an
'untouchable' in society. [55] The *dysfunctional Reformist* may well

---

[53] The only way of living acceptably to God was not to surpass worldly morality in monastic
asceticism, but solely through the fulfilment of the obligations imposed upon the individual by
his position in the world. That was his calling….the fulfilment of worldly duties is under all
circumstances the only way to live acceptably to God….moral justification of worldly activity
was one of the most important results of the Reformation.
Max Weber: The Protestant Ethic and the Spirit of Capitalism

[54] The rich man in his castle,
The poor man at his gate,
God made them, high or lowly,
And order'd their estate.
Cecil Frances Alexander, 1818-1895

tar beggars with the same stick as sinners, and withdraw into his shell of intolerant indifference, or even of outright hostility towards both.

Conversely, within Romanist society, the beggar is regarded in the Franciscan tradition as a suffering 'innocent' who, by definition, is close to the Lord; John and Charles Wesley, leaders of the evangelical revival in the Church of England and founders of Methodism, exhorted Christians to gain and to save all they could, in effect, to grow rich: then they added that these same Christians should *give everything they could to the poor*.

The monetary success that accompanies the pious man predestined to salvation supports the idea of government by the virtuous and wealthy, in that only those who have been obviously blessed by God's bounty, and who lead a sober life, merit the task of leading others. If a Christian is successful and frugal, his unspent wealth leads to the accumulation of capital, and, because he is predestined to salvation, unspent riches cannot be contrary to God's favour: this is the providential, sober interpretation of capital accumulation by the 'aristocracy of the elect,' that underlies the Weber Thesis. It is germane to the idea of the worldly saint that wealth not be used to support luxury or self-indulgence, and that money not be spent on personal pleasure. The protestant Bible states that, "the *hard working man* is thoughtful, and all is *gain*," (Prov. xxi v. 5.) which flatly appears to contradict the notion that it is good to be poor: desiring poverty in the Franciscan sense is like wishing for bad health;[56]

---

[55] O ye wha sae guid yoursel,
Sae pious and sae holy,
Ye've nought to but mark and tell
Your Neabour's fauts and folly!
Robert Burns: Address to the Unco Guid, or the Rigidly Righteous

[56] Benjamin Franklin himself, although he was a colourless deist, answers in his autobiography with a quotation from the Bible, which his strict Calvinist father drummed into him again and again in his youth: "Seest thou a man diligent in his business? He shall stand before kings" (Prov. xxii. 29.) The earning of money within the modern economic order is, so long as it is done legally, the result and the expression of virtue and proficiency in a calling;...
Max Weber: The Protestant Ethic and the Spirit of Capitalism

ironically enough, the Revised English Bible, which is used by Roman Catholics, translates this same quotation as, "Forethought and diligence lead to profit," appearing to pop the link between gain and *hard work*.

Although the accumulation of wealth is a direct result of the calling and of personal frugality, Reformist society accepts that money in itself constitutes a great danger: as fiery preachers have repeated from their pulpits, its temptations never end, leading to idleness, temptation of the flesh, and diversion from the righteous life. The calling is the commandment of the individual to work for God's glory, and it should inspire orderly conduct in the pursuit of duty, rather than spontaneous, impulsive enjoyment of its fruits; it gives a methodical character to asceticism. The English Empiricist philosopher, Bishop George Berkeley, summed this up by saying that life is *not* a struggle against rational acquisition but *against the irrational use of wealth.* John Wesley completed these remarks by saying that *"religion must necessarily produce both industry and frugality, and these cannot but produce riches: but as riches increase, so will pride, anger, and love of the world in all its branches."* In essence, the accumulation of capital should be balanced by a strong wish to "do the right thing" with it.

Reformist societies have a very different outlook on time from that of Romanist societies. Benjamin Franklin was probably the first to claim that '*time is money,*' and his position found comfort in the Calvinist idea that a man cannot atone for time lost in not working towards God's greater glory. It is a short step from this to conclude that waste of time is indeed a deadly sin.[57] Within Reformist society time is quantified: it can be wasted, saved or even killed. To save time in a meeting, the Reformist uses only inductive logic, gives only essential facts and answers only relevant questions; he is upset by the laborious Cartesian method adopted in Southern Europe, where deductive logic is used to gain

---

[57] Not leisure and enjoyment, but only activity serves to increase the glory of God…Waste of time is thus the first and in principle the deadliest of sins.
Max Weber: The Protestant Ethic and the Spirit of Capitalism

support before taking action. The Reformist requires people to be
on time and to give, and to respect, deadlines; agendas have to be
clear; goals have to be specified at the start to avoid losing time
further on: one has to "stick to business;" to "get to the point;" to
"cut the cackle," and to "define the deliverable." Meetings within
Reformist dominated cultures have to be short and decision
oriented: you don't waste a Reformist's time; you make it quick.
The Romanist is overcome with panic in such a meeting.

In summary, then, the sober and industrious Reformist finds
justification in worldly success: he believes that piety can mix
with business acumen, and profiting from God's bounty is not
encompassed in his idea of sin. Success in this world is a sign of
divine approval, and the Reformist does not dissociate virtue from
wealth. He has no complex about money, and has no wish to
mortify others about theirs: wealth can indeed be a sign of virtue
in this world, and, because God favours the industrious and the
good, there is no reason to hide it as long as he accumulates his
capital for the day when it will be needed to do God's work. The
Reformist hopes to recognise his salvation through hard work and
frugality; he is expected to lead an ascetic existence, and not to
spend his accumulated capital on personal pleasure. He must
develop a taste for temperance and for honesty.[58]

Reformism is considered to be 'this worldly;' dogmatic
proclamations, which are not rooted in 'biblical evidence,' are
rejected as meaningless; it is said to be 'linear,' because
Reformists take the Bible as the sole written authority for
Christianity and hold that doctrine must be logically derived from
it. John Calvin walked this path in facing an omnipotent God with
His omniscience and His omnibenevolence, and formulated the
only doctrine he could find within the compass of God-given
human logic, that of *predestination*. The Reformist inspects the

---

[58] For if that God, whose hand the Puritan sees in all the occurrences of life, shows one of His
elect a chance of profit, he must do it with a purpose...To wish to be poor was, it was often
argued, the same as wishing to be sick..."God blesseth his trade," is a stock remark about those
good men who had successfully followed the divine hints.
Max Weber: The Protestant Ethic and the Spirit of Capitalism

balance of his life regularly for confirmation of his predestined salvation; he has no truck with the catharsis of Catholic absolution. He can become sullen and pessimistic in his lonely submission to determinism; he finds the childish grin in contradiction with sober behaviour expected of a pious adult, and harbours suspicion of excessive emotion.

The dysfunctional Reformist's principles may degenerate into rigidity, and into a self-righteous distance that he places between himself and those whom *he* has judged as God's condemned: as his fear of being predestined to eternal damnation leads him to distance himself from the sinner, he risks falling into the traps of contempt; at best, intolerance, and, at worst, bigotry: he may privately pity the sinner as a condemned soul, but the risk of despising him also, is high.

He could well come to appoint himself the judge of the *"right thing to do,"* believing in a single universal morality, to be followed at any cost despite the collateral damage such stubborn ideals can so easily cause. The worldly saint would never accept that the end could justify the means; he would reject all forms of expediency on principle, and become outraged at mistruth in the mouths of those he has elected lead his community: he has no mistrust of plutocracy, providing that the elect are identified from among the manifestly virtuous: to become elders, he would hold that they must deserve the confidence their community has placed in them.[59]

If not as sullen as Calvinists, members of other protestant creeds are nonetheless more this-worldly than their Catholic cousins: as a Lutheran or as an Anglican, both creeds having historical roots

---

[59] (The creation of the Calvinist's own salvation) cannot, as in Catholicism, consist in a gradual accumulation of individual good works to one's credit, but rather in the systematic self control, which at every moment stands before the inexorable alternative, chosen or damned...The God of Calvinism demanded of his believers not single good works, but a life of good works combined into a unified system. There was no place for the very Catholic cycle of sin, repentance, atonement, release, followed by renewed sin.
Max Weber: The Protestant Ethic and the Spirit of Capitalism

in Catholicism, a Reformist may not necessarily fully lead his or her life under that Sword of Damocles, predestination.

The Reformist appreciates clear agendas and prefers short, disciplined, decision-oriented meetings. The dimension of time is quantified: it can be wasted, saved or killed; time is money; the waste of time is not in accord with the spirit of sober industry; the idea of respecting deadlines is within Reformist society 'the right thing to do.'

Sitting next to a Dutch woman at a dinner in early 2009, I asked her how, as a Dutch Catholic, she evaluated the impact of Calvinism on national behaviour. After explaining that the majority of Dutch Calvinists live in the East towards the border with Germany, and that she came from the West, she explained that she had had to change her behaviour in France: she had been too *direct* at first, and she had learnt to be less *abrupt*; she associated abruptness in her national character with Protestantism.

THE REFORMIST IN BRIEF

The precedence he accords to humanly perceived reality over dogmatic assertion, which appears unfounded in nature, leads him to be pragmatic, rather than dogmatic. He rejects thought not obviously rooted in empirical knowledge or in unquestionable, biblical authority, and argument that does not use linear, human logic. His or her thought processes are thus strongly <u>analytic</u> and scientific.

He is, as a result, suspicious of mysticism and of cathartic spirituality: he finds his spiritual solace in the individual practice of asceticism. He respects time and deadlines.

The Reformist submits to a fate predetermined from all eternity; he is pessimistic, relatively unsmiling, suspicious of the show of emotion, and he keeps his distance. To avoid dangerous association with sinners, he is watchful of others and sensitive to their virtue or lack of it; he is quick to judge them on the basis of his own inflexible ethic, and can slide into dysfunctional contempt and into intolerance.

The Reformist learns to follow the wisdom of the recognised virtuous elders of society, and he is deeply disturbed by any sign of their "unworthiness" to lead.

He believes that wealth can be the God-given, unspent fruit of individual, virtuous labour, and seeks not to stigmatise the rich because of their money.

CHAPTER 5

REPUBLICANISM

*...whoever refuses to obey the general will shall be constrained to do so by the whole body, which means nothing other than that he shall be **forced to be free**...*
Jean-Jacques Rousseau: The Social Contract

People think they have taken quite an extraordinarily bold step forward when they have rid themselves of belief in hereditary monarchy and swear by the democratic republic. In reality, however, the state is nothing but a machine for the oppression of one class by another, and indeed in the democratic republic no less than in the monarchy.
Friedrich Engels

Europeans and their neighbours have experimented with all sorts of republican models throughout history, from the ancient Greek city states to the medieval, bourgeois, Italian city states; from the creation by protestant emigrants of the United States of America to the creation by communist luminaries of the Union of Soviet Socialist Republics. The republican model, with its ancient pedigree, is nonetheless associated by its devotees with modernism and with social progress notwithstanding the collapse of the Soviet Union and the success of progressive constitutional monarchies throughout Europe.

The archetypal model of European contemporary republicanism is described with vigorous distaste for monarchy by the Swiss, Jean-Jacques Rousseau (1712-1778,) an obsessive anti-monarchist and a staunch missionary for utilitarian ideals of liberty and equality within a 'Social Contract.'

Rousseau found individual, feudal, monarchical power intolerable because the individual prince could manipulate the law to his own advantage. He wished no man to be another's master; he held that all men hold the inalienable, self evident right to freedom.[60] In this way, it becomes the objective of the collected citizenry to destroy despots and tyrants, who, instead of governing subjects to make them happy, "*make them wretched in order to govern.*" He distrusted authority, feared arbitrary rule and painted monarchy in such ugly colours that it took but a short while for the Guillotine to make its grotesque collection of French aristocratic heads. Rousseau's cynicism of monarchy led him to claim that "*truth is no road to fortune, and the people dispense neither ambassadorships, nor professorships, nor pensions:*" in effect, because the honest man could never benefit from the patronage of a prince, it could not be a duty to yield to a prince's will. He affirmed that, as the state is owned, and should be controlled, by its citizens, it cannot be governed by an individual monarch: the citizens must delegate the function of government to equals under a social contract, investing them with limited powers and extensive obligations. [61]

Faced with republican zeal at the end of the eighteenth century, the French monarch might well have countered that he had been *anointed* by God to occupy his exalted office, as his predecessors had been for centuries before him: unfortunately for Louis XVI, John Locke (1632-1704,) the English Empiricist philosopher, had debunked belief in the divine right of monarchy a century earlier. Furthermore, republican philosophers were sceptical of the way in which monarchy used religion to its advantage: no doubt *they* had read their Machiavelli on the subject, as paraphrased by Rousseau.

---

[60] If we enquire wherein precisely lies the greatest good of all, which ought to be the goal of every system of law, we shall find that it comes down to two main objects, freedom and equality.
Jean-Jacques Rousseau: The Social Contract

[61] ...ruling is a science that is least well mastered by too much practice; it is one a man learns better in obeying than in commanding.
Jean-Jacques Rousseau: The Social Contract

Rousseau affirmed that, "*whereas natural liberty is only bounded by the strength of the individual, civil liberty is limited only by the general will.*" Even Machiavelli, hundreds of years before, had claimed that what makes the people truly prosperous is "*not so much peace, as liberty.*" Rousseau thought that the only way authority could be legitimised between free men was on the basis of agreed, written convention. Because a free man can express himself as he wishes, freedom of expression is a fundamental sign of republican liberty; information is expected to circulate and to be shared between men because they are born, not only free, but equal.

On the other side of the Atlantic, Rousseau's contemporary, the English immigrant, Thomas Paine, had held high the banner of freedom from the British crown at the start of the American Revolutionary War in his pamphlet, 'Common Sense,' (1776:) as a critic of Edmund Burke's, 'Reflections on the Revolution in France,' and a student of John Locke, Paine wrote, 'The Rights of Man' in 1791. This influential figure helped to ensure that the fledgling America would embody the anti-monarchical ideals rife among European republican philosophers.

Rousseau's words were taken to heart by the Revolutionaries in France, who promptly stamped republicanism with the ideals of egalitarianism and fraternalism to give a foretaste of the 'Commune.' In fact, Rousseau affirmed that "*Government exists to maintain equality,*" which he defined as a state where "*power is never great enough for violence and always exercised by virtue of rank and the law.*" In his opinion, the republican has to work hard to maintain equality as, "*Circumstances always tend to destroy it.*"

Rousseau surmised that citizens acclaim individual liberty; personal security; mild government; crime prevention; disinterested neighbours, and bread for all. What values could better have challenged the concept of feudalism? If you offend a member of the Republic, you offend the body of the Republic: it is thus the goal of government to ensure what Locke called *"personal liberty with political order."* Although the individual is free, the state comes first; however, all free men who work in the interests of the state work in their own interest, and in the fraternal, collective interest. From here the 'fraternal' step to Socialism and to Communism is very short indeed. As fraternal collectivism implies informality, social equality, and quality of life for all, what ideal could be better adapted to the virtues of 'teamwork?' Furthermore, in a republic, work is not about profits, but about *employment.*

Rousseau declared that the majority that takes power by right, invariably has right on its side on the occasions of popular uprising: the *"general will is always right and tends to the public advantage because it tends to equality,"* whereas *"the particular will tends to partiality."* He justified revolution and civil war as necessary resistance to a feudal monarch, and went on to advise civil disobedience when government does not act in the interest of the people:[62] French citizenry have applied this idea ever since the creation of their republic; from the revolutions of 1789 and of 1848; from the Paris Commune in 1870, and from the student rising of 1968; to the strikes of its rail-company unions and to the recurrent street marches and demonstrations. The French take to the streets for two reasons: firstly, Rousseau advised them to; secondly, popular discontent shown in the streets is a tolerated part of political feedback by the citizenry to its politicians, who not only take notice, but act fast to resolve the problem; otherwise they lose votes, if no longer their *heads!* Politicians must react; if they don't, they not only alienate the protesters, but also the rest of society suffering from the protest: French citizens do not tolerate their 'parental' government allowing suffering among brother citizens; this is part of the ideal of fraternalism; as parents know, if one child starts crying, it's probable the its little brothers and sisters will start crying too.

---

[62] ...he who has command over men must not have command over laws, neither must he who has command over laws have command over men... Since no man has any natural authority over his fellows, and since force alone bestows no right, all legitimate authority among men must be based on conventions...
Jean-Jacques Rousseau: The Social Contract

More than a century before the French Revolution, Oliver Cromwell's republican 'Commonwealth' survived in England for ten years after axing Charles I's head in 1649: this act brought home to terrified continental sovereigns the threat of popular revolution at a time when any excuse was good enough to have one. Following the Reformation, the motives for revolution in Britain had *religious* overtones in that the *Puritan*, Cromwell, fought the *Anglican* monarch, Charles I; whereas, in France, the popular uprising was *politically* motivated by the struggle between the haves and the have-nots. In effect France, which had already destroyed Protestantism, underwent its renewal crossing the monarchical-republican divide of the French Revolution, whereas Germany, the Low Countries and Britain saw it crossing the theological divide of the Reformation.

As men are thought to be born equal, the class structure that exists within monarchy does not exist in a republic, where, in principle, informality is the norm; but if communications in the United States are informal, this is not so in France, where they remain coded, formal, sober, though egalitarian, as if the politeness of Louis-Philippe's court had been massaged into the Second Republic. Because education is the great leveller of society, the principle of equality requires the pauper's children to be as educated as the Prince's, and the pauper to be spoken to with the same deference. Today in France, 35 per cent of the French young go on to heavily subsidised higher education, coming from all walks of life and from all social strata with the possible exception of some of the first generation Maghrebian young.

The ultimate individual achievement within the republic is successful service to the state: status is attributed as a collective acknowledgement of accomplishment rather than by ascription by a prince or by his court. Rousseau insists that a republic rarely raises to the highest office men who are not enlightened and capable, and therefore, an elected head of state holds his position thanks to merit and talent: meritocracy replaces aristocracy, the Prince's feudal oligarchy; capacity and personal worth on the job are more effective criteria of choice of rulers than succession, despite any claim that princes are bred to the position and educated from the earliest years to assume leadership of their state. This is why France (like other European republics) is governed by its star pupils from the 'great schools' such as the, "Ecole   Polytechnique,"   or   the   "Ecole   Nationale d'Administration," and a handful of others. The elected President is expected to be virtuous and capable, tough, knowledgeable, clever, a leader and a visionary. He can aspire to almost monarchical status, but only during his or her period of office. The republican complains that a monarch can reign even if he is a waster and has 'flunked' school.[63]

The humanism of republican thought sidelines religion from state affairs; it endows the state itself with quasi-divine attributes and encourages its citizens with nationalistic fervour and devotion to national icons, such as to the flag: there is no royal family to read about in the press, nor to mourn with, as Britain mourned Princess Di.[64] A spiral of religious prejudice and of anti-clericalism can develop when a state replaces God, leading it to 'sanitize' religious influence in the education of young republicans. In 1882, the French republican politician, Jules Ferry, passed a seminal law in France making education, "free, *secular* and compulsory:" France passed a law in 1905 separating the Church from the State, and continues to pass legislation, such as in 2005, to remove *religious ostentation* from the garments of schoolchildren. The lay Republic provides fertile soil for ideals of humanism; the 15th century Dutch humanist, Erasmus, inspired much of Rousseau's work.

---

[63] An essential and inevitable defect, which will always make monarchical government inferior to republican government, is that, whereas, in republics, the popular choice almost always elevates to the highest places only enlightened and capable men, who fill their office with honour, those who rise under monarchies are nearly always muddled little minds, petty knaves and intriguers with small talents…a man of real merit is almost as rare in a royal ministry as a fool at the head of a republican government.
Jean-Jacques Rousseau: The Social Contract
[64] Although Nicholas and Carla Sarkozy's couple has achieved "presse pipol" (sic) status and sold a lot of magazines.

The Pantheon in Paris looks like a church, but it is unconsecrated; housing Foucault's pendulum, it is also a monument to the quasi-divinity of the state; the crypt hosts the mortal remains of the visionary Voltaire and Rousseau a few metres from each other: ironically, they detested each other in life. Other eminent republicans, sympathetic to certain anticlerical values of the French state, are inhumed there too.

Napoleon was an upstart, talented Corsican soldier, who became a very able administrator during republican development in France. In May 1804, some 15 years after the republican French Revolution, he had himself crowned Emperor! What could be more monarchical? He launched his 'Civil Code' in March of the same year: it remains, with its revisions, intact to this day as a massive, explicit document ordering the law in every walk of life down to the last "Cartesian," tortuous, hair-splitting detail. Putting decisions in writing is a characteristic of republicanism, from the works of Plato to the legalism of the United States: the written word is given ultimate authority because, as power is intended to be collective, putting it on paper protects the population from the arbitrariness of a powerful individual. It is not surprising that it was the French who attempted to draft a constitution for the European Union in 2005: Valéry Giscard d'Estaing called it the "Convention," to avoid obfuscating the monarchists, who probably didn't want a written European constitution at all; it's not difficult to understand that, if a country such a Britain has no written constitution of its own, it is not going to be happy about having its hand tied by one imposed on it by "foreigners." In fact the final version was so watered down that it read more like a letter of wishes; it was more surprising that the French, in a national referendum, voted it out over domestic issues. When the Irish Republic did the same thing a few years later, the French president, who was presiding the European Union, asked them to go back and vote again! He might have added, this time, "properly!" More about this in Chapter 8.

France's Romanist ethic 'runs on steroids' when merged with its republican 'equal and fraternal' tradition. The French social system has taken protection of society's weak out of the hands of the individual Frenchman and institutionalised good works under the state banner of republican fraternity. The French squeeze the wealthier half of the working population to support a generous welfare state, and hardly tax at all the income of the poorer half: the rich individually seem to donate less to charities, than in societies where collective paternalism towards the poor is less organised. As well as the abolition of aristocracy and of individual privilege, today's republic wields such tools as *'fiscal justice'* to level individual wealth. Heavy death duties and wealth tax permit the government to redistribute wealth from the richer to the poorer classes in long term interest of creating an egalitarian state.[65] France is one of the few countries to maintain a wealth tax, and does so despite the seeming unfairness of taxing capital constituted by income that has already been taxed; despite pressure even on right wing, majority governments to remove it, none has had the courage to do so in the face of the national outcry it is likely to cause; as monarchy will not protect the nobles against the people, republics will not protect the rich. John Locke claimed that *labour* is the origin and the justification for property, whereas princes inherit their property: according to him, inheritance does not justify property at all, and republicans dislike it because it works against equality; wealth taxes are, after all, effective tools to apply Locke's thoughts. The Statue of Liberty stands in Manhattan with its younger and much smaller sister overlooking the Seine in Paris: would not twentieth century France have done better to call her the 'Statue of Equality?'

At the time of writing, the rich French are the possibly most heavily taxed nationals in Europe, and their money looks very much like fair game, both under Jean-Jacques Rousseau's

---

[65] ...no citizen shall be rich enough to buy another and none so poor as to be forced to sell himself ; this in turn implies that the more exalted persons need moderation in goods and influence and the humbler persons moderation in avarice and covetousness. (Do you want coherence in the state? Then bring the two extremes as close together as possible; have neither very rich men nor beggars, for these two estates, naturally inseparable, are equally fatal to the common good; from the one class come friends of tyranny, from the other, tyrants. It is always these two classes which make commerce of the public freedom: the one buys, the other sells.) *Jean-Jacques Rousseau: The Social Contract*

republican ideology of equality, and the Roman Church's implicit condemnation of the demon, money. They become 'tax refugees' to Britain, to Switzerland or to Belgium: London was in 2007 the third largest 'French city' in the world with hundreds of thousands of French nationals living there, many of whom are France's most talented youths, who should be at home building their country for the next generation. Too much taxation destroys taxes.

Plato in his 'Republic' states that he wished to purge Greek poetry of any encouragement to selfish or to uncooperative behaviour; he thought that competitive individualism is one of the most important problems of society. People enjoy their wealth alone: they have no desire to share it with others. He wished to reform politics and education to foster the ideal of a citizenship, where citizens seek to *share* with their fellows. In this way, the Republic would function harmoniously as a whole and not as a succession of minor conflicts. As much as Rousseau distrusted rich men, he distrusted beggars too: *"from the one,"* he claimed, came *"the friends of tyranny, and from the other, the tyrants:"* extremes of wealth in society are dysfunctional. He claimed that *"luxury ... corrupts the rich by possession and the poor by covetousness."*[66]

The republican social pecking order is not money based, but based on service to the *State*: it is honourable to serve the State, and it follows that honour is bestowed by the *State* on the individual. The State assumes an overriding persona: for example, the French Police technically are less responsible for serving the public than the State: the mission of the French National Police, quoted from the first article of its 'Code of Deontology,' is to *"guarantee the freedom and the defence of republican institutions, to keep the peace and public order, and to protect persons and property."* The concept of *serving the community* in the sense of

---

[66] ...for luxury is either the effect of riches or it makes riches necessary ; it corrupts both the rich and the poor ; it surrenders the country to indolence and vanity ; it deprives the state of all its citizens by making some the slaves of others, and all, the slaves of opinion.
Jean-Jacques Rousseau: The Social Contract

the London 'Bobby' or of the street-corner 'Chicago Cop,' would appear to be absent.

There is nothing to confirm that republics are more 'modern' or more democratic than European constitutional monarchies. Monarchs generally reign for life, and, when they die, are succeeded by a relative, whereas presidents of republics are generally elected for a limited term, and their successors chosen by election. Whether it be a constitutional monarch, or an elected president, both are subject to the law and to their constitutions. Owing to the fact that the President of a republic is elected on a political platform, if his party holds a parliamentary majority, he wields far more power than a constitutional monarch. Nicholas Sarkozy is much more powerful politically than Queen Elizabeth II; in fact he has been accused of excessive centralisation by his ministers; Barack Obama has the power to order international military intervention in the teeth of Congress; there is no way Queen Elizabeth II could do such a thing; for a political ideology that is intended to protect the people from arbitrary *individual* power, and that considers monarchy pre-modern, republicans may not necessarily be *totally* convinced by their presidential model.[67]

The 18th century political theorist, Montesquieu, distinguished three forms of government: the republican, monarchical and *despotic* models. His concept of the monarchical model was equivalent to today's constitutional monarchy, and that of the despotic model to feudal monarchy or to dictatorship. Montesquieu thought that "monarchy has honour for its object, republic has virtue, but despotism has fear." There are no feudal monarchs left in Europe, but if we extend his idea of despotism and fear to the present day, we discover republican despotism that had been unknown to him because, as yet, not invented: the

---

[67] Any state which is ruled by law I call a "republic," whatever the form of its constitution; for then, and then alone, does the public interest govern and then alone is the 'public thing' – the *res publica* – a reality. All legitimate government is 'republican.'
Jean-Jacques Rousseau: The Social Contract

Communist Party machine of the now discredited Soviet Union; the National Socialism of Hitler; or Mussolini's Fascism.[68]

Vatican power broking played its age old-role in precipitating the downfall of Soviet-Socialist *Republican* communism: Pope John Paul II supported the Polish 'Solidarity' movement in the early 1980's and paved the way to 'Perestroika' and to the destruction of the Berlin Wall in November 1989. By then, 71 years of communism and two wars had brought Russia and the Eastern European republics to their knees: Communism had inculcated a tradition of apathy, laziness and fear in the hearts of its citizens, and sacrificed three generations of happiness and freedom.

The repressive machinery of Soviet communism treated dissidence in much the same way that the Church treats heresy, that is to say, by 'excommunication.' The Prague Springtime of 1968 is a tragic example: managed by a visionary but possibly naïve leader of the Czechoslovakian Communist Party, Alexander Dubcek, he relinquished control of his country's media by allowing the abolition of censorship when Leonid Brezhnev was the General Secretary of the Russian Party: public ecstasy and pandemonium followed. May 1968 saw cathartic riots in Paris and a popular move to institutional change, but Prague's freedom to change was illusory: August of that year saw the massing of Soviet troops at the Czechoslovakian frontier; the Russians and their German Democratic Republican friends had been dismayed at the rise of *"counter revolutionary"* pressures and at the risk of discovering *"American imperialistic insurgence"* among the Czechoslovakian people. Prague's heady springtime didn't last a day longer than the time it took for the Russian tanks to occupy the streets of the capital, and Dubcek was "excommunicated" from the Party: after 20 years of friendship with Brezhnev, he was demoted to a junior administrative job in the Ministry of

---

[68] A Republic is a nation in which, the thing governing and the thing governed being the same, there is only a permitted authority to enforce an optional obedience. In a republic, the foundation of public order is the ever lessening habit of submission inherited from ancestors who, being truly governed, submitted because they had to. There are as many kinds of republics as there are graduations between the despotism whence they came and the anarchy whither they lead. *Ambrose Bierce*

Agriculture, isolated and forgotten; one of his senior women colleagues was 'repositioned' as an office cleaner.

As Soviet-Socialist *Republican* communism, born of the ideology of Marx, Engels, Trotsky and Lenin, had its excommunicates, so also it had its martyrs: in 1918, for example, its adherents murdered the Tsar, Nicholas II, and the six other members of the Russian royal family: 90 years later, Russia was licking its wounds and trying to piece its broken past back together, when, in 2008, it amassed its tanks again, this time along the Georgian border. However, would the oligarchs who managed the Union of Soviet Socialist Republics be totally absurd in "yah booing" that other vast Republic, the United States of America, in its military adventures in Korea, Vietnam, Iraq or ironically, the object of their own demise, Afghanistan?

The highest calling in the Republic is to serve the state, which embodies the will of the people, and not that of any individual: excessive power held in the hands of an individual is viewed with suspicion because it opens the door to arbitrary rule. This is the philosophical basis of the republic, and the fact that presidents of certain European republics today hold greater constitutional power than contemporary European monarchs, appears to attest to the weakness of the republican principle in the face of political opportunism. The state is divinised, and its children are commemorated in its Pantheon, erected to keep the clerics of this or that denomination in their place: the republican is wary of clerical interference, which he has ever identified as the foremost tool of monarchical influence over the people.

The republican takes the utilitarian view of the collective interest coming before that of the individual, and 'wears his heart' on the collective side rather than the individualistic side of his coat.[69] It

---

[69] Each one of us puts into the community his person and all his powers under the supreme direction of the general will: and, as a body, we incorporate every member as an indivisible part of the whole…the private will inclines by its very nature towards partiality, and the general will towards equality.
Jean-Jacques Rousseau: The Social Contract

is because the power is invested in the people that citizens must
be kept informed; otherwise it cannot properly exercise its
collective mandate: spontaneous sharing of information, widely
communicated in all its forms, whether written or verbal, must be
volunteered and be made available. The republican is not
compulsively secretive in his communications, and exercises his
unquestioned right to ask questions to gain understanding.

The exercise of power by the people requires a forum that is, from
time to time, wider than that of a parliamentary debating chamber:
elected deputies are there only through the mandate of the people;
so, when there is unresolved social discord, the classical
republican takes to the streets to vent his frustration. This taste for
civil disturbance is viewed by parliament with 'republican'
equanimity as the voters' prerogative, but less so when it
degenerates into the level of civil disobedience capable of
producing social upheaval, as France has seen repeatedly in 1789,
1848, 1870 and again in 1968. In all things, however,
republicanism respects the collective right to publically manifest
discord, and looks upon public demonstration as a safety valve or
as a cleansing agent.

As the people are made up of the collective of individuals, there is
no reason to consider that any one member of the public should
be placed in a position of power or of status above any other,
except, perhaps, in the exercise of invested authority on behalf of
the people by an elected individual. The republic does not in
principle distinguish between princes and paupers, and both
fosters and protects the equality between all citizens. To the
republican, the idea of equality appears self evident; not so to the
monarchist.

Republics do not desire the class structure of monarchies, so for
purely ideological reasons, they may tolerate a little class war
from time to time. If all men are equal, then there is no reason to
adopt the formal manners designed to protect and to isolate the
Prince; you do not speak to a prince on equal terms; and, whilst
good manners must subsist to 'oil the wheels' of communication,

the formality can be removed in a republic because there are no class barriers. Informality defends the values of equality and favours relaxed, forthright communications and direct contact; it is the hallmark of certain republics, such as the United States of America or Finland, but not of all: the formality remaining in the manners of certain European republics, such as France and Austria, is a monarchical throwback, perpetuated through each country's particular brand of 'monarchical nostalgia' of the coming and going of monarchy and republic throughout the nineteenth and early twentieth centuries.[70]

Despite fruitless colonial attempts by England, France and Spain, the United States has never accepted monarchy, whereas every European nation except Switzerland has been one for many centuries at one time or another. We would be extremely surprised to find monarchical sympathies among Americans, as monarchy is absent from their political compass. What passes for 'republican' attitudes and behaviour in the American 'Grand Old Party' appear to have rather less to do with the politics of Rousseau, than with the morally absolute ethics of Reformism, dysfunctional or not. The United States have never united under a monarchy, and have a *foreign* idea of monarchical values in society: for example, the American conception of republican liberty is quite different from the French one, which really was formulated to resist the pauperisation of a people following a millennium of feudal reign and disastrous economic management by the monarchy. American liberty does not exist today in opposition to feudal monarchy, but searches to protect individual prerogative, whereas French liberty protects the collective from individual monarchical power: one extols the freedom of the citizen, and the other the freedom of the collective from the individual; when, in a radio interview of a striking French university researcher in February 2009, she commented that the movement was resisting measures which had been *arbitrarily*

---

[70] An aristocracy in a republic is like a chicken whose head has been cut off; it may run about in a lively way, but in fact it is dead.
Nancy Mitford

imposed by the government, she and her colleagues were expressing the fundamental understanding in France of the word, "liberty."

In essence, then, European republican equality brings the state to assume the mantle of judge between the haves and the have-nots in application of the accepted doctrine of the destruction of inequality of wealth: this contradicts the monarchical principle of the protection of individual wealth. As only half of the working French pay income taxes, a special definition of equality applies before the tax man. The republican, from his or her school days on, is brought up to internalise the need to support the weaker elements of society, and considers it a self evident mandate of government to take from the rich to give to the poor: as inheritance works against equality, European republican law tends to legislate against the accumulation and the protection of dynastic assets; private asset destruction has been the definitive tool of destruction of aristocracy since the French Revolution.[71] As assets are destroyed, so is privilege, and Thomas Paine affirmed that privilege by birth ends with a whimper in a generation or two. It is little wonder then that the 'dysfunctional' rich in a republic take great care to hide their wealth and to distrust the propensity to legalise pilfering of their assets; the republican ideal lies clearly at the root of that of the Welfare State, which thrives under fraternal approval of the republican mission to protect the poor as underprivileged members of the community.

If, historically, power has been in the hands of the aristocracy, the destruction of this class of society and the appropriation of its privilege and capital to the utilitarian, collective good, leads the republican to search for leaders from other spheres to administer the State: the fact that certain individuals appear to have more leadership qualities, or vision, or mental capacity, than others, has

---

[71] Grant me thirty years of equal division of inheritances and a free press, and I will provide you with a republic.
Alexis de Tocqueville (French Historian and Political scientist. 1805-1859)

led the republic to lay its hands on the best and the brightest; meritocracy replaces aristocracy; the mandate is given to those who can, rather than taken by those who have. Academic performance is the key to finding future leaders from the earliest age, and republics institutionalise the recognition and the development of exceptional minds; from Napoleonic times, the brainiest have been taken early by the hand and led through education into positions of influence; the late bloomer rarely makes it in the administration of a European republic, where youthful talent and academic pedigree remain the most effective passports on the road to public success. In this way, the republic uses *merit* as the vector which replaces feudal aristocracy with the presumption of the greater efficiency of meritocracy.

As King John discovered at Runnymede, the written word, duly signed and sealed, carries greater weight than the spoken one: while monarchies have struggled throughout history to avoid its chains, republics have always harnessed its constraining power to lock in change and to afford reasonable protection of the collective from the tyranny of the individual. The republican takes the written word very seriously indeed, and applies it far more extensively than the monarchist: Napoleon, despite his imperial ambitions, wrote the first French Civil Code through a perceived need to define the law: it has been expanded by successive republics into dozens of tomes and tens of thousands of pages with every conceivable variation of law and of public administration provided for, in flat contradiction, as we have seen, with the equity of English law based on a statute book, precedent, the absence of a written constitution, and, in the tradition of King Solomon, exceptionally wise High Court judges.

As moral absolutism pervades religious thought, so it pervades republican sentiment: how else would the collective hue and cry have been strong enough to justify mass ritual murder by the Guillotine of the French aristocracy from 1792? According to the official figure, 17,500 people were guillotined between 1792 and 1795: despite this, republicans are deeply convinced of the superiority of their political system in 'modern' society, even with respect to constitutional monarchy.

Republicanism cohabits well with Roman Catholicism, as is illustrated by the 45% of the 433 million Europeans, analysed in the data used for this essay, being Catholics living in European republics.

THE REPUBLICAN IN BRIEF

The Republican idealises the state, and gives it a humanistic, quasi divine personality: the divinisation of the state does not easily harbour the 'other' divinity of religion, and the dysfunctional Republican might show anticlerical tendencies. He holds that the utilitarian collective interest comes before individual interest, and he champions the concept of equal status for all.

In the absence of 'monarchical nostalgia,' there is no room for individualism nor for careful formality in his or her behaviour: he or she is distinctly collective or <u>communitarian</u> in his or her values.

The Republican may hold a morally absolutist view of the 'modernism,' and, implicitly, of a superiority of the republican model over the monarchical one, constitutional or not, which can border on political intolerance.

The imperative of the fraternal redistribution of wealth appears to him as self evident: one that the Republic reinforces in schoolchildren from their earliest age. He mandates government to ensure equality of opportunity for all members of society and to 'fraternally' redirect collective resources to the support of the weaker members of society.

He is wary of individual power held outside the circle of his elected leaders, whom he has chosen on the basis of merit and of recognised talent, and he attributes little honour to those who show commercial success: business leaders, who are unelected, who hold economic power, and who accumulate individual wealth, never benefit from the kudos of those who devote their professional lives to the State, and thus to the good of all.

The Republican expects information to be spontaneously shared and encourages debate to gain understanding. He sees little need for confidentiality outside state security, and regards civil disturbance with equanimity, because it is an acceptable and expected social outcome of his political opinions.

CHAPTER 6

RECOGNISING CARICATURES

Subjects prize public tranquillity; citizens, the freedom of the individual;
the former prefer security of possessions; the latter, security of person;
subjects think the best government is the most severe; citizens that it is the
mildest;
the former want crimes to be punished; the latter want them prevented;
subjects think it good to be feared by neighbours; citizens prefer to be
ignored by them;
the former are happy when money circulates; the latter demand that the
people have bread.
Jean-Jacques Rousseau: The Social Contract

As all Europeans live either in a monarchy or in a republic, and in
societies with more or less Romanist or Reformist majorities,
their behaviour and attitudes are influenced by a political and a
religious vector. Each vector includes a proportion of monarchist
behaviour and attitudes, and a complementary proportion of
Republicanism, and each religious vector is closer to a binary
choice between Romanist behaviour and attitudes on the one
hand, and Reformism on the other; although Reformism clearly
opens onto a multiplicity of theologies ranging from Anglo
Catholicism to ascetic Calvinism.

In searching to establish cultural stereotypes, I use caricatures of
individuals who religiously and politically find themselves at the
poles: caricatures are extremes by definition, and the probability
of finding a person whose behaviours and attitudes are squarely
located at an extreme is statistically very small indeed, so I hope
the reader understands that what follows is a guideline of the way
individuals can be, rather than as a generalisation of the way they

are. The outcome applies to no-one in particular, but hopefully caricatures many in general.

Sketches of behaviour and attitudes provoke defensiveness in all of us; we claim that, *"we are not like that at all*!" I suggest, then, that it would be most useful to read about the way *others* are and to compare our conviction of *how we believe they are*, with what is written about *them;* this in the belief that, understanding why others are different, we would rather be sympathetic to diversity than critical of it!

I have no doubt that virtue and dysfunctionality in each European draws him or her naturally to a balance between the interests of the collective and of the individual on the one hand, and between the mystical and the pragmatic on the other, just, some, *"more so than others*!" Where political and religious influences tend to cancel each other out, I consider the characteristics of society to be *balanced*: one such case is the strongly collective ethic of Romanism being countered by the strongly individualistic behaviour of Monarchy: otherwise said, in a country such as Spain, the concern for the welfare of others, which is so strong in Romanism, compensates to some extent the individualism of class-conscious, monarchical society. A similar balance is found in the United States, Finland or Iceland, but, in this case, it is the individualism of Reformism that is to some extent balanced by the ideal of the republican collective.

Politics and religion can also have strong interactions, because their paradigms can reinforce each other with synergic effect: for example, the effect of Reformism on Monarchy may lead to isolated, highly individualistic, ascetic behaviour, and even to xenophobia or contempt for those of other nations.

Conversely, the synergic effect of Romanism on Republicanism leads to the compulsively classless, collective behaviour, which we might see in French society, the home of equality and fraternity; France provided the fertile ideological ground for the development of socialism in the late nineteenth century.

The interactions of Monarchical, Republican, Romanist and Reformist paradigms on behaviour and attitudes exposed in this essay have four important combinations:-

i. Romanist/Monarchical called, **ROMMON**
ii. Romanist/Republican called **ROMREP**
iii. Reformist/Monarchical called **REFMON**
iv. Reformist/Republican called **REFREP**

I have summarised the political and religious combinatory characteristics of each under three headings:-

a) Privilege

Privilege is a special right, advantage, or immunity for an individual or limited group of individuals, which others do not have, including the right to say or to write something without the risk of punishment by a superior power such as the monarch or the state. Individual privilege of one can be more or less acceptable to other individuals according to their social paradigms, and typically accumulates increasingly to the benefit of the privileged individual as he rises through the social layers of a class system.

b) Aggregation and Egocentricity

From the Latin verb, *aggregare*, which means to 'herd together;' aggregation is the tendency in certain societies to give priority to collective ideals over individualistic ones. Egocentricity is the tendency for individuals to centre on their own interest at the expense of the interest of others, or of society in general, and can be tinged with suspicion, with mistrust and with aggressively self-centred behaviour called 'machismo,' which is the behaviour resulting from strong or aggressive masculine pride, the word being derived from the Mexican Spanish *macho*, meaning 'male.'

c) Thought process

This heading describes the process by which ideas and opinions are produced around religious and political convictions: it leads to a 'paradigm,' which is a system of ideas, or a conceptual model, of the theories and practice of society and which is the frame of reference by which an individual constructs his model of behaviour and attitudes. The process may use deductive,

'Cartesian,' reasoning, with a tolerance for un-provable dogmatic premises, to build a paradigm based on elliptical thought; or use inductive logic with pragmatic reasoning to derive a paradigm based on linear, empirical reasoning.

After each model, is introduced an imaginary European, middle class, university-educated, 45-year old professional, whose behaviour reflects the stereotypes: Juan lives in Madrid, the capital of Spain, an ancient monarchy, where Catholicism was the *state* religion until 1978; Giovanni, an Italian republican living in Rome, the home of the Vatican and of Roman Catholicism; Johannes, living in Amsterdam, the capital of the Kingdom of the Netherlands, and a member of the Dutch Reformed Church, which is, with the Presbyterians, the largest Calvinist community in Europe; and Jean, a republican from Geneva, Switzerland, which is the home, (apart from San Marino,) of the oldest republic in Europe, and the birthplace of Calvinism.

ROMMON: The Romanist/Monarchical model
a) ROMMON Privilege
The respect the ROMMON learns for clerical hierarchy interacts with the individualism of monarchy to favour the layering of his society into classes; class barriers within his community protect privilege and limit contact. Those who *have* power and privilege appear gracious, formal, tactful, diplomatic, discrete and aloof; their concern is the institutional protection of their personal property, of their status, of their rights of inheritance, and of staying informed through their network. They have little compunction in making decisions in the interest of convenience. Their power is protected both by the tradition of monarchy and by the teaching of the Church, whose clerics exhort the faithful to virtue by respecting the *rights* of others and by doing their *duty* by others. The inferior class individual's concept of politeness is that of discrete formality, of acquiescence and of inoffensiveness to avoid disturbing others; he respects others' privacy without expecting to enter into their confidence, but he craves patronage which he expects in return for personal service. Towards his social inferiors he acts like those who *have* power and privilege.

b) ROMMON Aggregation and Egocentricity

The individualism of monarchy is balanced by the collective ideal of Romanism and helps to avoid the excesses of each: the ROMMON, who acts in his best self interest and relies on himself rather than on others, congregates naturally with others to contribute, for example, to charitable work. The self-centredness of monarchical society may be reinforced by the Romanist *'emotive' machismo* that the male child may carry into adulthood: in the Freudian sense, the power of the Romanist, matriarchal female adult is compensated in the ROMMON by an excess of 'emotive' male-child self assertion; such behaviour is accepted in their men by young female members of ROMMON society, who become tomorrow's matriarchs. Emotive machismo is at times characterised by self indulgence, externalisation of moral responsibility onto the shoulders of others and, in some cases, a weak sense of duty; the ROMMON may tend to make *convenient* decisions; he may not necessarily keep his promises; he may claim the right to change his mind and may not own up to misdemeanours; he may not apologise nor admit to error; he is unafraid of sin and carelessly optimistic. He can be self-centred, isolated, mistrustful of others, and may have no doubt that the end *can* justify the means.

c) ROMMON Thought process

The ROMMON is likely to tolerate unproven, dogmatically formulated premises and is happy to discuss them for hours using Cartesian scepticism. He can be capable, in his choice of premise, of elliptically rejecting observed experience in favour of dogma, so his life may not always be guided by thoughts which conform to observed facts, and is accordingly the consummate artist. He may feel some discomfort with wealth and an emotive, mystical relationship with the divine. He may well find it unimportant to respect timelines.

Meet Juan (ROMMON)

Juan is a factory manager who works in the outskirts of Madrid running a factory of 1,000 people. He is secretly proud of the status his job confers in the local community, and of the reputation that his boss, the successful CEO of his company, is forging for himself in the national press. Juan is a royalist: he was delighted to witness the reestablishment of the Spanish monarchy from 1975 after the death of the military dictator Franco, and believes that the country was returned to its rightful, historical rulers; he says that the House of Bourbon has never let Spain down. He believes meritocracy to be unnecessary in the position of a head of state because royal succession confers all the legitimacy that is necessary. In his work, good order dictates that a boss, whatever his talents, or lack of them, must be obediently followed.

His friends are important to him because they all come from his own professional class; they confirm his position in society and ensure that he knows what is going on around him. He has been trying to convince his wife to invite a bishop they know to one of their dinner parties at home: the Church is a useful hub for their social contacts, and there is no reason not to take advantage of it, but he is not convinced that the great man will accept his invitation. He does not like surprises and has stopped investing in the stock exchange; he buys 'triple-A' government bonds instead. Preoccupied with his position in local society, Juan feels uncomfortable with his poorer neighbours, whom he faintly mistrusts and whose problems are not his concern; he feels no more at ease with his boss's rich friends, but their acquaintance might be useful; Juan would like exposure to, what he calls, the "right circles," and regrets being excluded from them. He cares above all else about his own welfare and happiness and for that of his family; he prefers to do a job himself than to trust others, who invariably get things wrong; he sees himself as a loner and admits to suspicion of others. He is relieved when the political party in power takes its greedy eyes off his wealth and possessions, which are rightfully his and his family's, and should never be fair game for a rapacious state.

At work, Juan's words never lead to confrontation, and he adds discrete manual and facial gestures to precisely communicate how he feels. He respects refined manners in others, and is irritated when they are not as deferential, seemingly harmless and diplomatic as his own. Juan is polite, knows how to charm, is always formal, and rarely smiles. He discusses tactfully, keeps his facial expression under control, tries never to show emotion and keeps his voice confidentially low, but, on the rare occasions when irritation gets the upper hand, then he explodes in anger, which happens in the family, but almost never at work.

An essential part of his job is negotiating employee benefits with the works council, where he deeply believes he has a duty to improve the lot of the factory operators. He knows labour law quite well, and, though not a lawyer, Juan enjoys showing that he masters the ins and outs of this complex subject. He gets deeply involved in detail during meetings, taking the time necessary to discuss questions to the satisfactory understanding of all: the meetings go on into the night, and he rarely gets to his dinner appointments before 10 P.M. He uses the remote formal form of the second person singular at all times in the office, and feels annoyed and offended at the use of the familiar form by some of the younger workers.

Juan attends mass every Sunday with his family, and follows the sermons carefully: the priests are saintly and experienced men, who know how to listen and to give advice. He says that they are fortunate to be able to spend their lives serving God, and that, without the temptations or distractions of the everyday life of the layman, he is sure that it must be easier for them to practise virtue. Sometimes he imagines himself as a monk, and thinks that, if ever he were to find himself alone in later life, he might join a monastery. He is confident that the Church will guide him down the road to salvation, just as promotion will result from doing a good job for his boss. Besides, he does not believe for one moment that an indulgent and good God would wish to condemn him to eternal hellfire. He admits to being mischievous, and, as time goes on, he refuses himself less and less. The luxury car he drives is his pride and joy: it was ridiculously expensive, and he gave some money to the Church when he bought it, to appease God, so to speak, for such a "sinful" acquisition.

The factory workers don't earn much money: Juan believes that they have been less lucky in life than he, and that their financial suffering in this world earns them, no doubt, a better chance of getting to heaven than his. He is sure that their union representatives don't always speak the truth, and certainly not if it's not in their interest to do so, so he doesn't overreact when his staff lies to him: he knows that they expect him to lie back from time to time: it's all part of the game. They understand too that he is not going to keep a promise unless it suits him, and that to do so is his prerogative as the boss; of course, he never leaves anything in writing. Juan realises that convenient solutions are not always the most ethical ones, but if they cause less trouble, then he never hesitates to use them. He also admits to not thinking it appropriate to befriend his direct subordinates.

ROMMON

Solitary-isolated-
    secretive-networker
Formal - Hierarchical
Class; property; status-
    conscious
Optimistic-Self Indulgent
Mistrustful
Intolerant-Dogmatic
Expedient-changeable
Emotional; macho
Elliptical-Cartesian-
    deductive
Disregards time
Synthetic-artistic

In the family, Juan enjoys conversation, going to museums and visiting churches. He takes his mother with the rest of the family when he can, knowing how much she appreciates anything religious.

ROMREP: The Romanist/Republican model
a) ROMREP Privilege
On the one hand, republican politicians tend to divinise the persona of the collective and to promote classless equality between society's members, exalting the superiority of collective power over individual power. On the other hand, dysfunctional Romanism may foster the idea of the weak, child-like self protected by the priestly hierarchy of powerful, 'mother' Church. As a result, the child-like ROMREP finds himself submitting to

two powerful collectives; to a notional, divinised state and to a divine, matriarchal Church; this 'double whammy,' may place him in a position of child-like dependence on the collective; citizens are equally inferior before the state and equally children before the Church. The paternalistic Republic interacts with a matriarchal Church to cultivate not responsible, adult, but dependent, child-like citizens. If the collective vents its frustration on the streets in child-like manner, the ROMREP may view the resulting civil chaos with relative equanimity, because he sees not responsible adults, but brothers and sisters; children of the State. The ROMREP spontaneously shares information; there is no privilege to protect, so there is no reason for secrecy.

b) ROMREP Aggregation and Egocentricity
The foremost protagonist of socialist and communist politics, the classless ROMREP draws his preference for the mutual good from the fraternal-egalitarian ethic of the Republic and from the 'family of the faithful' aggregation of the Roman Church. He is a natural team worker and perfectly able to place the interest of the common good before his own. He is an active team contributor, ready as a Cartesian to debate to improve his understanding, and careful as a republican to recognise merit and talent in others. Romanist maternalism and republican fraternalism balance any individualistic tendency the ROMREP may have. Unafraid of sin, optimistic, emotive and sometimes anticlerical, he is likely to attribute responsibility to others, rather than to himself, and not to own up to misdemeanours. Convinced of the superiority of his society, his Romanist machismo could be tinged with a dash of intolerance, but any self indulgent, dysfunctional, child-like, expedient behaviour he may have is balanced by an outgoing, fraternal ethic. The ROMREP does not reject the principle of the redistribution of wealth to the poor and the duty of the state to appropriate it from the rich; so those ROMREPs, who have riches, are likely to hide them, knowing that financial success confers no status in their society and that their wealth, inherited or not, may ever be fair game for the State.

c) ROMREP Thought process
The dogmatic nature of Romanism and the scepticism of its followers can lead the ROMREP to think elliptically and

deductively. The other-worldliness of Romanism and the republican ideal may lead him to easily internalise un-proven, morally absolutist premises: he learns to reject human experience in favour of dogma; he accepts mysticism and discovers catharsis; he may attribute a quasi divine personality to a secular state, and deduce his own position of inferiority to it; he may feel guilty about individual wealth and believe time to be unimportant in the vast scheme of creation. He can rationalise inconsistency with human experience by using elaborate, deductive thought; with Cartesian style, he may learn to derive elliptic conclusions from unproven premises. He finds no barriers to creation; he is synthetic in his thinking, and an artist.

Meet Giovanni (ROMREP)

Giovanni believes ardently in Italy's republican constitution; his grandfather had never been complimentary of the Italian monarchy, the House of Savoy, after Mussolini's fall from power, and had prided himself on joining the Resistance during the War. He spends many evenings at his local Socialist Party office, where he is responsible to the executive committee for union affairs. He supports the unions at all their demonstrations, and takes the kids with him to march to the music if it's a fine day and to whistle and jeer with the crowd. He feels righteous about humbling the rich and the powerful, and he instinctively distrusts most forms of authority. Giovanni enjoys the heady comradeship of the other "intellectuals," a number of whom he has known since his bearded university days, and he hopes that the children will follow his political lead, as Giovanni followed his grandfather's.

It seems obvious to him that the State's function is to protect the weak, care for the poor and to destroy poverty: society relies on the State to look after its members from the cradle to the grave, and responsibility for the wellbeing of each of its citizens must not be individual, but collective. Because the values of a republican state can only ultimately be virtuous, Gianni believes that service to his country confers status, so, he has chosen a

RECOGNISING CARICATURES

career as a civil servant. His job is probably for life with lots of
free time to follow his interests: he knows he will never be rich,
but he cares less for money than for his profession: administrative
detail and procedural content are his areas of competence. He gets
deeply involved in his work, and is convinced that the longer a
meeting lasts, the more satisfactory its outcome. He is not worried
about respecting deadlines or about making last minute changes
to his diary.

He inherited a little money from his grandmother: it's sleeping in
a bank account "just in case." He believes his mother, who attends
Mass every morning, is a saint, and echoes her words in claiming
that "poverty is close to sanctity;" he believes that his deceased
father, who was a physician, had led a good life because he had
been more concerned about helping the poor and the sick than
about earning extra money for his retirement. They had never
spent much time together.

He uses the familiar form of the second person singular in
addressing his office colleagues rather than the formal address,
which he finds old fashioned and stuffy, but after years of public
service, he chooses his words carefully so as to properly convey
subtlety of meaning. Giovanni uses flamboyant manual and facial
gestures to communicate complex and emotional content in his
words. If he gets excited, his tone of voice rises and his body
language becomes more pronounced, but this is both normal and
necessary; without it, he knows that his colleagues won't believe
he really means what he says: in fact, if he gets really excited, he
throws diplomatic caution to the wind, and "let's fly." Giovanni
cheerfully admits to openly showing the gamut of his emotions;
"Sometimes, it's the only way around here of getting anything
done!" he says.

He gets a kick out of serious conversation in the family,
discussing art, visiting churches, and soccer, which is the only
time he spends with his kids, who are, he says, his wife's
territory, and not his.

Giovanni listens carefully to priestly teaching on Sundays; he claims that the Church knows what's best. He likes the younger priests, whom he finds quite aware, although, along with his Party friends, he feels faintly suspicious of the institution of the Church. He appreciates the feeling of release he gets from going to confession and knows that, as a human and as a sinner, he will return repeatedly for more despite his fleeting, good intentions not to sin. He says that, "to err is only human," and believes that God is an understanding and pardoning Father to all his weak children. He is optimistic that he won't be eternally damned: all he has to do is to follow the sacramental rule, and providing he goes to Mass on Sundays, there is probably not much more he needs to do about his soul. Like his mother, he admires the asceticism of contemplative monks and the mysticism that surrounds their life, but he would not wish to emulate their self discipline. He feels vaguely guilty that he is not doing anything directly useful to help the poor and the hungry, and hopes that his work with the union compensates this.

ROMREP

Fraternal-Team Worker-
  Egalitarian
Information sharer
Informal-Dependent
Utilitarian-Childlike
Optimistic-Carefree-Self
  Indulgent
Chauvinistic
Expedient-changeable
Emotional; macho
Dogmatic
Elliptical-Cartesian-
  deductive
Disregards time
Synthetic-artistic
Discomfort with money

He admits with a grin to being slightly mischievous and self indulgent, particularly over food. He is baffled by the idea of owning up to wrongdoing, which he finds naive, because people should only tell the truth if it is in their interest to do so: he has no qualms about confessing to a priest, but sees no reason to confess to anyone else.

REFMON: The Reformist/Monarchical model
  a) REFMON Privilege
The monarchist isolation within class barriers to defend privilege is heavily reinforced by the REFMON's introspection; he

RECOGNISING CARICATURES   111

functions best in an ivory tower, hierarchically isolated from others; he respects his place in society, asks that others respect their own, and attempts to befriend neither his superiors nor his social inferiors. He reasons that benefiting from individual privilege is perfectly acceptable, and acts with subservience towards those from whom he expects patronage. The REFMON is watchful for the signals of speech, accent, loudness or tone of voice; for non-verbal signals; and for the forms of politeness, which mark the class barrier between himself and others. He ascribes status to the upper classes and is sensitive to his exclusion from their society. If he feels superior, he will appear gracious, aloof, confident; if not, he will appear harmless, confidential, discrete, formal, tactful, and diplomatic. The REFMON treats information on a need-to-know basis: adept at the use of secrecy, he learns of what is occurring from his own information network. He aggressively protects his rights, and expects the state to protect his property and his inheritance, and *not* to redistribute it to other classes of society, poorer or not.

b) REFMON Aggregation and Egocentricity
The isolation of the REFMON within his class enhances a tendency towards introspection and asceticism, but brings him to aggregate easily with others of his own class in clubs and in associations; he or she can become a solitary, isolated adult, relatively inflexible in his or her opinions, who associates virtue with self denial. He probably has no wish to work in a team, and believes he can get the same results simply by using the hierarchy. He relies on himself rather than on others, and is watchful of both; he defends his own and his family's interest above and beyond any other, and in all circumstances; the collective probably having no recognisable personality in his life, it lacks the importance the ROMREP gives it. Monarchical isolation reinforces the suspicion he harbours of others and may incite censorious behaviour. The REFMON is fatalistic, pessimistic and suspicious of emotion. He can be self-centred, preoccupied with his status and with his state of spirituality; he can be obsessed with the need to isolate himself from sinners, from foreigners and from the lower classes, none of whom he takes much interest in. He protects the right to change his mind in

his own interest and in that of his family; he can believe that the end justifies the means, yet he can be equally tortured by his duty to do the right thing: in the case of misjudgement, he may neither admit to error, nor apologise for it. Quick to judge and to condemn, skilful in irony and a master of understatement, the REFMON can slide easily into dysfunctional contempt, xenophobia and intolerance.

c) REFMON Thought process

The pragmatic, this-worldly outlook particular to the Reformist gives the REFMON a linear, inductive style of reasoning; following his monarchical inclinations, it links simple logic with expediency and combines a practical ethic with self-serving individualism; as a result, he may be challenged by doubt over the 'right thing to do.' More comfortable with fact than with opinion, and irritated by laborious, deductive argument, especially if it is based on tenuous dogmatic premises, the inductive REFMON's empirical mind can tolerate error: he is happy to be only 'mainly right' because it's action that counts. He is suspicious of mysticism and of catharsis; he respects time and deadlines.

Meet Johannes (REFMON)

Johannes is a tax accountant working in Amsterdam for eminent businessmen in the city. He is sensitive to the fragility of his small business, and works hard to make his firm profitable.

He discusses the subject at hand without deviating from the point, and remains relatively unsmiling throughout. He dislikes hypothetical conversation and is impatient with what he calls, "fuzzy" thinking. Johannes is polite, sullen, lofty, formal and tactful. He speaks in a low voice so as to appear harmless, approaching others discretely and confidentially, and he acts with impeccable manners. His friends say that he is obsessively prudent, secretive and over controlled; his French acquaintances perceive him as austere, abrupt and ironic.

He spends little time in meetings but ensures that it is spent efficiently, just walking out if progress is not made. He quantifies time: time is money; time is lost or gained; time can be wasted, sinfully so!

Johannes is proud of his wealth, believing it to be the result of hard work and of self denial. He is not ashamed of his money and sees no reason to hide it: he is, however, careful about how he spends it: it may be the fruit of virtuous labour, but it should not be the tool of self indulgence, so Johannes tries to be frugal by spending little on personal pleasures. He hates wasting money, and only grudgingly approves of charity to the poor, harbouring more than a mild suspicion of those whom fortune has not favoured. He is deeply introspective and, like his father, often mulls over his behaviour. He carefully avoids those who have shown signs of less than perfect probity and those who are too lazy, or too loud, or who laugh, or spend, too much. He fears to associate with wrongdoing or with those who perpetrate it: Johannes flees obvious sinners, and admits to faintly despising them.

He believes that the State's paramount duty is to protect the personal freedom and possessions of its citizens imposing the rule of law and order. He has a strong regard, not only for his rights, but also for his duties within society. He is impatient with disrespect in all its forms, and is an isolationist, suspicious of foreigners.

He associates only with those whom he trusts, and whose loyalty has stood the test of time. He protects his wealth and interests through association with others of his class. Johannes clearly recognises those from other social classes and accepts that there are barriers to communication and to friendship; he navigates comfortably within his own class, but not in others. He cares obsessively about his family's safety and financial security: a member of influential associations, and of one of the most exclusive Golf Clubs in Holland, he frequently exploits his personal network of contacts to promote his firm's business. He sees no reason to "team up" with others rather than relying on himself, and does not buy into all the hype in business about 'teamwork.' He believes that it is just a way to cover up the inexperience of junior management.

He is cynical about his social inferiors and tends to avoid them, but he is deferent to powerful and successful individuals: Johannes is anxious to be included in the "right' circles, and dislikes exclusion from them. He believes in the rights of monarchy and in the duties of subjects towards it, providing, of course, that the monarch is virtuous. He thinks some monarchs good and others less so, but sees no reason to modify the ancient right of succession: the House of Orange-Nassau has always provided the country with dignified heads of state and, although he suspects that he will never meet a member of the royal household, he points proudly at his orange Princeton shield, where he spent a year at the university as a graduate student; he wonders how many at the university associate their colour with Dutch Protestantism.

REFMON
Solitary-isolated-
   secretive-networker
Aloof
Class; property; status-
   conscious
Pessimistic-Mistrustful
Intolerant-censorious
Self-serving, expedient
Suspicious of emotion
Duty bound
Pragmatic
Fact based-Empirical-
   Inductive
Respects deadlines
Comfortable with money
Action oriented

He has seen expediency in action many times during his career, and grudgingly accepts that it is necessary: he tries to be pragmatic, knowing that the truth is not always told, nor promises always kept; he is nonetheless disturbed by lack of rectitude on the part of community leaders, who really ought to set an example. He thinks that such behaviour is, unfortunately, pervasive in society. That a member of the royal family should behave in such a way would be, for him, unthinkable.

He mistrusts clerics and feels slight contempt for "supernatural nonsense;" disliking what he calls, "magic," he associates this with "mystic" religion. Johannes finds his comfort and refuge only in the eternal, and unchanging, biblical texts.

REFREP: The Reformist/Republican model
a) REFREP Privilege
The Republican ethics of fraternity and egalitarianism confer a desire for classless equality on individuals in REFREP societies. REFREP society gives priority to the utilitarian collective good over the individual good; its citizens are wary of individual despotic power; although state interest comes before that of each individual, every citizen is attributed equal status before it. Citizens communicate with each other informally and spontaneously, sharing information. Government accepts civil disturbance as the rightful expression of its citizens when the collective of citizens disputes decisions.

b) REFREP Aggregation and Egocentricity
Lonely Reformist morality, which encourages introspection, is balanced by the collective ideal of Republicanism; the REFREP learns that the collective comes before the self, and so believes that the common good comes before the individual good. The suspicion of the Reformist and the anticlericalism of the Republican are balanced by the REFREP's collective, fraternal ethic; he may be suspicious both of sinners and of clerics and quick to judge others; indeed, he may slide into a dysfunctional attitude of intolerance, believing that his social model is *universally* applicable. He is isolated within his religious convictions and he values a life of individual, 'lonely-adult,' rather than 'child-like,' behaviour. He is watchful, not only of others, but of himself, and not particularly flexible in his attitudes, but he is prepared to debate in order to improve his understanding. He does not stigmatise the rich because of their wealth, and appreciates merit and talent in others. He attributes some status to commercial success. He can be tolerant of 'fraternal' redistribution of riches to the poor by institutional appropriation of private assets. He keeps his promises and is extremely upset if others do not do so too; he is likely to own up in the case of misdemeanour. He feels discomfort with the show of emotion and is both fatalistic and generally pessimistic.

c) REFREP Thought process

The pragmatic, this-worldly outlook, which is particular to the Reformist ethic, leads the REFREP to think linearly and inductively; he exhibits a pragmatic, this-worldly, if pessimistic outlook; he is empirical, more comfortable with facts than with opinions, and suspicious of arguments which he finds illogical or not in accordance with his own perception of reality, particularly if they are mystical or peppered with emotional 'undertow.' He believes in the universal *"right thing to do at all costs,"* and is very likely to spontaneously own up to his misdemeanours. He respects his deadlines and looks upon the State as a virtuous and exemplary organism.

Meet Jean (REFREP)

As a lawyer, Jean is an active participant in his community. He has had a successful career because he works long, diligent hours; he says he has to work hard to counter competition from other firms all fighting over the same clients, and to improve the performance of his own firm, which is specialised in "ethical business," and which is located in the centre of Geneva. He has no qualms at all about the very large sums of money he invoices his clients, and has cultivated such an indifference to it that those, who don't know him well, underestimate his wealth. Like his father, he has always tried to spend little on personal pleasure, and, despite the size of his bank account, he admits that he hates wasting money; he profoundly dislikes idleness in himself and in others, and, outside his work, he can think of very few activities that are not ultimately a waste of time and money.

He is obsessively honest and reliable in his work, and feels strongly that all professional individuals within his community ought to give the example of virtue: if they don't feel the weight of social responsibility on their shoulders, then they are not true professionals. As an outside, wizened observer of European-

Community politics, he distrusts political potentates, and insists that those who are responsible to the community must deserve their status, as most of those who have been elected to the Swiss Cantonal governments have managed to do since the institution of the Confederation in 1848. Jean is outraged by the idea that convenience could justify wrongdoing or mistruth in positions of public responsibility. He has an inflexible regard for the law, and despises those who don't; as a lawyer, he has to carefully hide his distaste for defending clients in criminal cases; on one occasion, he admits, he was so disgusted with the depravity of the accused, that he found another lawyer to represent him; on another occasion, he was ousted by an Italian client for "arrogance!"

He believes that a collective state does embody the virtues of society, and that individual service to it is the duty of every citizen; this is why, even at 45, he cheerfully does his three weeks of military service every year. He accepts that, in order to function properly, the State must have a rightful claim to a part of his assets, and he does recognise the primacy of state interest over his own. It is the job of the State to protect the weak, to look after its citizens, and to come to grips with poverty: Jean gives a little money, though grudgingly, to charities he has carefully chosen for their strongly ethical behaviour.

REFREP

Fraternal-Team Worker
Information sharer
Informal -Egalitarian
Utilitarian
Pessimistic-Watchful
Intolerant, isolated adult
Suspicious of emotion
Universalist; "right thing to do"
Pragmatic-debates to understand
Fact based-Empirical-Inductive
Respects deadlines
Analytic-logical
Comfortable with money
Action oriented

He navigates within an extensive professional middle class, and, he is quite interested in the views of vocal, minority interest groups.

He mistrusts institutionalised religion, and shows stubborn suspicion of what he calls "mystic religions," which, he says, are basically superstitious. He dislikes flamboyancy in church and is impatient with, what he calls, "fuzzy theology," and which he defines as not being of strict biblical origin: Jean considers himself to be a "religious pragmatist," and finds all the religious guidance he needs in the Bible.

He is an avowed pessimist, and only rarely smiles. Nervous of excessive formality, he is well mannered; he never 'embroiders' language, and he is very 'direct,' both at the Bar in court, and at home; he speaks on equal terms, without compromise or deviation, remaining largely expressionless throughout; he hates showing emotion, and feels little comfort in its show by others.

Jean quantifies time: time is money; time is lost or gained; for him, waste of time, like waste of money is sinful. He carefully controls the time he spends in meetings with his clients, and always ensures that time is efficiently spent and that progress is being made. He invoices every second he spends with his clients.

CHAPTER 7

DEMOGRAPHICS AND THE GRID

At the end of the 19th century, France, already into its third Republic since 1789, was the largest of the only three European nations to have a republican constitution: the other two were Switzerland and the city state of San Marino; but a surge of republicanism followed the destruction of the Austro-Hungarian and Russian monarchies during the 1914-1918 Great War; more than twenty Austro-Hungarian, and ten Russian, kingdoms, principalities and grand duchies, had disappeared from central and Eastern Europe by the end of the hostilities.

In the sample[72] of European countries analysed in this essay, in 2007 there were 233 million professed Christians living in republics and 113 million living in monarchies; 87 million persons (20% of the population) did not declare themselves as Christians. The population living in republics outnumbered that living in monarchies by two to one, and Catholics (254 million souls) outnumbered Protestants (92 million souls,) by almost three to one.

Figure 1 shows that 45% of this population are ROMREPs; this single category is more than the sum of ROMMONs (14%,) REFMONs (12%) and REFREPs (9%,) put together, which add up to only 35%.

Of the total of the twelve European monarchies in existence on going to press, ten are constitutional: this is to say that the

---

[72] Table 1; Appendix A

monarch has little or no say in the politics of the state. Some are kingdoms and some are principalities.[73]

Today's Europe is divided into states with populations more or less sympathetic to monarchical or to republican values. The weighting used in Table 1 to grade each country on a Monarchical/Republican scale ought perhaps to be strictly binary, but a more precise idea is given by using a variable: I have used a "soft" one, I call, *'monarchical nostalgia,'* which is measured by the number of years since the disappearance of monarchy in republics weighted by the power and reputation of the ex-royal family. The Windsors, Hapsburgs and Bourbons are considered to hold more weight, for example, than princelings of the small German principalities, and the Belgian monarchy, which is quite recent, is given less weight than the ancient Spanish one; much also depends on whether constitutional change has occurred within living memory or has been long consigned to the history books: the disappearance of the Hapsburgs from the Austro-Hungarian imperial throne in 1917 was within living memory of my grandfather, who fought in the Great War, whereas the demise of the French Bourbons, which effectively dates from Louis Philippe in the mid 19th century, has been forgotten by all but French aristocrats; Austria is thus held to have greater monarchical nostalgia than France; furthermore, a national royal family may or may not benefit from national affection or from a high international profile; a foreign potentate may be viewed with different affections than a local one.

Monarchical nostalgia does not necessarily infer that a people wishes to restore monarchy, but that society has organized groups of the old aristocracy to remember their lost privilege; the people of Austria today show fondness for the unforgotten refinement of their deposed Hapsburg royalty: debutante balls in Vienna;

---

[73] They are: *the Principality of Andorra; the Kingdom of Belgium; the Kingdom of Denmark; the Grand Duchy of Luxembourg; the Principality of Monaco; the Kingdom of the Netherlands; the Kingdom of Norway; the Kingdom of Spain; the Kingdom of Sweden, and the United Kingdom of Great Britain and Northern Ireland.* The two not considered to be strictly constitutional monarchies are the *Principality of Liechtenstein* and the *State of the Vatican City.*

Chapter 7 Fig. 1: Proportions of Political-Religious Groups in the European Population

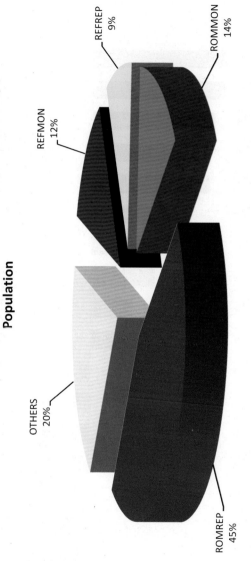

REFREP
9%

ROMMON
14%

REFMON
12%

OTHERS
20%

ROMREP
45%

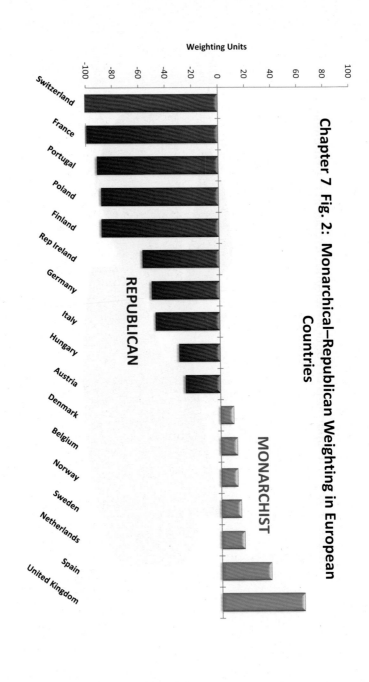

Weighting Units

Chapter 7 Fig. 2: Monarchical–Republican Weighting in European Countries

REPUBLICAN

MONARCHIST

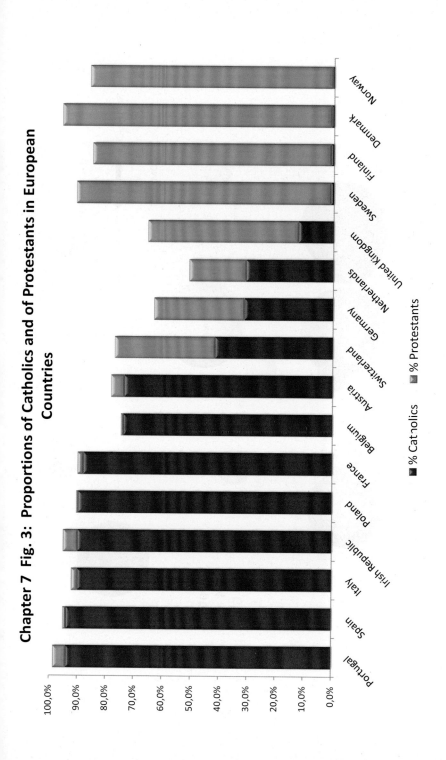

Chapter 7   Fig. 3:   Proportions of Catholics and of Protestants in European Countries

■ % Catholics   ■ % Protestants

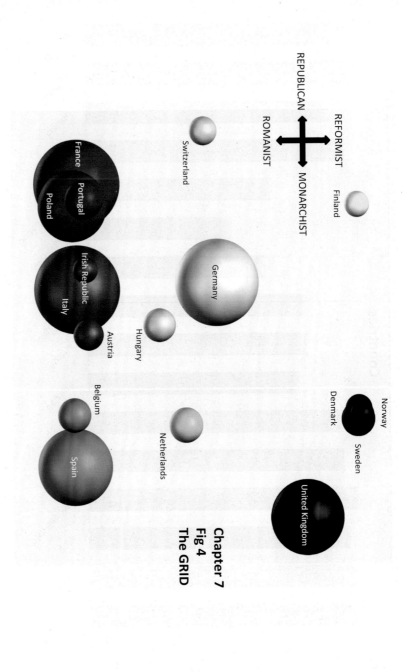

Chapter 7
Fig 4
The GRID

REPUBLICAN

REFORMIST

ROMANIST

MONARCHIST

Switzerland

Finland

France

Portugal

Poland

Irish Republic

Italy

Austria

Hungary

Germany

Belgium

Netherlands

Denmark

Norway

Sweden

Spain

United Kingdom

fascination with the old aristocracy; strongly conservative politics and pride in a magnificent architectural heritage all attest to the survival of monarchical sympathies within a state that lost its monarchy almost a century ago; even the French, after all this time, have active aristocratic associations such as L'Association d'Entraide de la Noblesse Française, to help out impoverished aristocrats, or La Société des Cincinnati, interestingly enough, with an active American arm, to bring together the military aristocracy that supported the Americans in throwing the United Kingdom out during the American Revolutionary War.

Republican states *do* get 'monarchical nostalgia,' and monarchical states are tempted by republican ideals, but, as long as the constitution remains stably monarchical or republican, I have assumed that the centre of gravity of national sympathy aligns to a point within the *existing* constitutional 'cocktail.

The only case of reinstatement of a major monarchy within European living memory is that of Spain, but in all other cases, monarchies have been replaced with republics.

These factors, some hard and some soft have been used to calculate a 'Mon-Rep Weighting' in Table 1, which searches to model the constitutional sympathies of the chosen European states. It is an approximate indicator of constitutional attitudes, from the most republican to the most monarchical, *and without any pretention of analytical rigour*: the list is not intended to be exhaustive, and the order does not arise from any precise science. Among the larger countries in the sample, Figure 2 shows France on the left with a strongly republican stance; Germany, with pockets of monarchical nostalgia, and Italy are in the group of young republics; the United Kingdom and Spain appear as the most monarchical nations. Switzerland has the most established republican sympathies; Austria is among the youngest republics, and the Scandinavian and Benelux monarchies complete the monarchical group.

Despite their doctrinal proximity to Catholicism, their Byzantine origin excludes Orthodox countries from the sample; also excluded are: those nations which espoused Islam during the Ottoman occupation of the Balkans; the Baltic; very small principalities and republics; and the heavier pre-1989 communist, Eastern European states. The model is in this way restricted principally to the traditionally Catholic and Protestant post-Reformation democratic nations of Western Europe.

Figure 3 shows that European countries have widely varying numbers of Catholics and Protestants: the difference between the percentages of the populations of Catholic and Protestant faiths, and 100%, gives the balance of all other faiths and of professed agnostics. The four Scandinavian countries on the right are very strongly protestant, and the eight very strongly Catholic ones on the left are those of Southern Europe with Poland, the Irish Republic and Belgium. Germany, Switzerland and the Netherlands have relatively balanced, if geographically distinct, populations of Protestants and Catholics.

Germany shows different doctrinal weights between its regions; Catholic Bavaria being culturally distant from protestant Hanover and from the Northern administrative divisions. The federal system of the Länder, however, appears to protect the country's unity against cultural explosion into the complex of pre-1918 kingdoms, principalities and grand duchies.[74]

The Netherlands, closely followed by Germany and the United Kingdom, appear to have the lowest proportions of professed Christians in their populations, with only 51% of the Dutch declaring themselves as such. European countries have experienced a decline in church attendance, as well as a decline in

---

[74] These included, Anhalt ; Baden; Bavaria; Brunswick; Hesse and by Rhine; Lippe; Mecklenburg-Schwerin; Mecklenburg-Strelitz; Oldenburg; Prussia; Reuß; Saxe-Altenburg; Saxe-Coburg and Gotha; Saxe-Meiningen; Saxe-Weimar and Eisenach; Saxony; Schaumburg-Lippe; Schwarzburg-Rudolstadt; Schwarzburg-Sondershausen; Waldeck and Pyrmont, and Württemberg; all of which had been unified under the Prussian 'Iron Chancellor,' Otto von Bismarck, in January 1870.

the number of people professing a belief in God; particularly, it would appear, among the Protestant nations.[75]

For the nations shown, 'The Grid' in Figure 4 plots their degree of Catholicism/ Protestantism with that of Republicanism/ Monarchism to see how they cluster. The size of each sphere is proportional to the total population of professed Christians in the country; the vertical axis places Romanism at the bottom and Reformism at the top, whilst the horizontal axis places Republicanism to the left, and Monarchism to the right.

Clusters of countries do emerge that appear to share similar cultures. We can identify, for example:
a) **REFMON**: the three Scandinavian countries appearing with the United Kingdom as the Protestant monarchies;
b) **ROMMON**: Spain and Belgium showing up as historically close Catholic monarchies;
c) **ROMREP**: republican, Catholic France, Italy and Poland forming a culturally influential 'tri-pole;'
d) **REFREP**: Finland appearing remote from its European neighbours, Scandinavian or Germanic.

Certain countries sit close to religious or constitutional divides, and can be described, if appropriate, using modified coding:
e) **ROM-X**: Austria and Hungary hugging the constitutional divide on the Catholic side;
f) **REP-X**: Switzerland remaining resolutely republican with a balance of creeds;
g) **MON-X**: the Dutch monarchy sitting across the Protestant /Catholic divide;
h) **REF-X**: there appear to be no significantly Protestant countries balanced between the constitutional models;
i) **X**: and finally, squarely occupying the middle ground, republican Germany, the complex home of the Reformation and of so many of the pre-1918 principalities, now of the Länder, appears to be the most pluralistic of the European countries, both

---

[75] For a discussion, see Appendix B

from a religious and from a constitutional standpoint. However, for simplicity I describe Austria as ROMREP; Switzerland and Germany as REFREP; and the Netherlands as REFMON.

The nationals of clustered countries could be expected show common behaviour and attitudes, which would tend to facilitate communications between their countrymen; and, whereas, opposites do sometimes attract, the *cultural extremes* clearly occupied on the Grid by France and England would testify to centuries of hostility, although this is not the case, to my knowledge, across the other diagonal from Spain to Finland. In fact, the United Kingdom would appear to be culturally remote from virtually all of its European Community partners, not excepting its historically independent neighbour, the Catholic, Irish Republic, but excepting possibly Sweden, Denmark and Norway.

Countries with balanced populations of Catholics and Protestants, such as Switzerland, Germany and, to far a lesser extent, the United Kingdom show regional cultural differences: Switzerland is made up of geographically distinct, Catholic, French- and Italian- speaking Swiss citizens in the Valais and in the Ticino, and protestant, German-speaking Swiss in the rest of the country; the North of Germany is mainly protestant, and the South, especially Bavaria, mainly Catholic; the United Kingdom shows regional differences of language and of religion between Anglican England, Presbyterian Scotland, Non-conformist Wales and mixed Northern Ireland. The nationals of these countries repeatedly speak of regional behavioural traits that appear to separate rather than to unite.

As the republican or monarchical choice of a *state* is binary, so is the Christian religious choice of an *individual* to be Catholic or Protestant; as a result, *any European Christian*, according to national constitution and to individual creed, *can place himself or herself on the Grid*. This has to be done with caution, though, because he or *she lives in a dominant culture that may not be his or her culture of origin or of preference*; furthermore the Grid oversimplifies the religious dimension of Protestantism by choosing only the extremes of the Catholic/Calvinist divide; Protestant Christianity is itself rich in different movements, potentially lending much more complexity to the model, but three years living in the United States taught me to "keep it simple!" The best I can suggest is to search to position one's creed somewhere along the vertical axis with ascetic Protestantism at the top and Catholicism at the bottom. By the same token, one's intimate conviction of the constitutional value of Republicanism and of Monarchy would lead one to position oneself accordingly on the horizontal axis.

CHAPTER 8

USING THE GRID TO UNDERSTAND BEHAVIOUR

European cultural influence has reached into many areas of the globe, and justifies to some extent applying the Grid to nations that are not geographically European: for example, Americans appear to be archetypal REFREPs, because, unlike European REFREPs such as the Finns or the Icelanders, whose protestant populations are in majority Lutheran, Americans had a dominant 'Mayflower' component of Calvinist immigrants at the defining moment of the Declaration of Independence: in addition to the English Puritan founding fathers themselves, active colonies existed of Scottish Presbyterians; of Dutch of the Reformed Church, who colonised Manhattan; of German Pietists and of numerous Swedish Lutherans who colonised the Mid West. Thomas Paine truly understood the roots of his country when he said in his pamphlet, Common Sense, *"The Reformation was preceded by the discovery of America, as if the Almighty graciously meant to open a sanctuary to the persecuted in future years, when home should afford neither friendship nor safety."*

It was among the Anglicans that the largest number of loyalists to the British Crown was found. After years of resisting the Catholicism of Quebec and the attempt to introduce Anglican bishops, the New England protestant ministers set out to enunciate the doctrines that became the basis of the American Revolution and of the Declaration of Independence. In the years that followed independence, with Quaker leadership, America brought together its protestant factions under a single defining, and, ultimately, influential movement.[76]

The United States shows a significant "Latin" population, which today to some extent counteracts the Mayflower influence: its tradition is an old one: the Vatican held its 1551 Council in *Lima*, and its 1555 Council in *Mexico*, both hot on the heels of the Council of Trent, which marked the triumph of Protestantism, and which preceded the sailing of the Mayflower by over 60 years. Both Peru and Mexico today could conceivably be described as ROMREPs; in fact, most of the South American continent could probably be described as such. Catholicism is also pervasive in the United States thanks to the Irish immigrants to the Mid West and to New England, but for all that, the American caricature remains fundamentally Reformist.

There is no reason, in similar fashion, not to extend the Grid to the Australians; to the New Zealanders; to white South Africans and to other communities; for example, Russia, rediscovering the Romanov graves, *canonising* murdered members of its defunct royal family, and taking a serious shot at updating its Republic, looks arguably ROMREP too, with more than just a hint of monarchical nostalgia.

Within Europe itself, France is the model ROMREP state because, despite Voltaire's atheistic writing and France's subsisting anticlericalism, the country still styles itself as the 'eldest daughter' of the (Roman Catholic) Church and is the quintessential European Republic born of revolution; Britain is the REFMON, and Spain the ROMMON, of reference.

---

[76] "I abhor two principles in religion and pity them that own them...The first is obedience to authority without conviction; and the other is destroying them that differ from me for God's sake."
William Penn

European behavioural caricatures in summary

REFREP	REFMON
Fraternal-Team Worker Information sharer Informal -Egalitarian Utilitarian Pessimistic-Watchful Intolerant, isolated adult Suspicious of emotion Universalist; "right thing to do" Pragmatic-debates to understand Fact based-Empirical-Inductive Respects deadlines Analytic-logical Comfortable with money Action oriented	Solitary-isolated-secretive-networker Aloof Class; property; status-conscious Pessimistic-Mistrustful Intolerant-censorious Self-serving, expedient Suspicious of emotion Duty bound Pragmatic Fact based-Empirical-Inductive Respects deadlines Comfortable with money Action oriented
ROMREP	**ROMMON**
Fraternal-Team Worker-Egalitarian Information sharer Informal-Dependent Utilitarian-Childlike Optimistic-Carefree-Self Indulgent Chauvinistic Expedient-changeable Emotional; macho Dogmatic Elliptical-Cartesian-deductive Disregards time Synthetic-artistic Discomfort with money	Solitary-isolated-secretive-networker Formal - Hierarchical Class; property; status-conscious Optimistic-Self Indulgent Mistrustful Intolerant-Dogmatic Expedient-changeable Emotional; macho Elliptical-Cartesian-deductive Disregards time Synthetic-artistic

The Grid is an entertaining tool to analyze relationships and events. If understanding ourselves and others better disposes us to sharpen our listening and to adapt our behaviour to that of others, then it must improve the sum of John Stewart Mill's 'utilitarian' good. As a European, I can position myself on the Grid; I can use it to predict which of my values is likely to separate me from another European I am to meet because, if I know his nationality, I can *start by expecting* from him the stereotypical behaviour and attitudes of his countrymen. Beyond the evaluation of personal behavioural interactions, the Grid also provides a useful framework to evaluate *collective* behaviour across nationalities.

Understanding such caricatures is the key to proper communication because it leads us to search for common cultural ground: for example, would a Northern European really grasp at the outset what ex Italian President Giulio Andreotti really meant when he reputedly said something to the effect that his country only ever became governable in times of crisis? Asking an Italian such a question over dinner might provide some fascinating insights.

There is no reason not to expect a paradigm shift in an individual who has spent a formative part of his life outside his native culture: an Italian who passes most of his career abroad modifies his or her behaviour and attitudes to assume the behaviour he or she admires in the culture of his or her chosen country. I believe that when a ROMREP goes to live in a REFMON state, his greater understanding of cultural difference will make him a far more effective communicator across cultures but possibly more of a cultural 'mongrel' for his acquaintances. As a person dilutes his own cultural base to integrate another one, he or she becomes an 'unknown' both in the culture of origin and in his or her chosen culture; an object of interest rather than one of intimacy. The person who is a Protestant but who admires Roman Catholicism and who is a Monarchist, but has a lot of good to say about Republicanism, may well be accused of lacking any opinions at all! Seeing all sides of the story makes one less vocal, less easily identifiable and an object of suspicion!

In 2008, tens of millions of investors worldwide lost money through the financial greed of the big American banks and the regulatory freedom they had won under the George W. Bush administration. The Subprime crisis occurred in a Reformist context, where it is probably all right to make lots of money and where the definition of *liberty* is that of the unregulated freedom of the pioneer. The banking industry succeeded in convincing the Securities and Exchange Commission to lighten regulation of their debt-to-capital ratios.[77] High Street banks were encouraged to sell mortgages to already indebted, high risk individual borrowers[78] losing sight of the bad risk profiles that would disappear in the bundling, or 'securitisation,' of such debt into funds; the banks sold and resold these funds again and again to take advantage of the leverage they afforded in generating more and more profit and larger and larger bonuses all round.

According to the International Herald Tribune of the 4th October 2008, a 55-minute discussion was held on 28th April 2004 between five commissioners of the SEC and five senior executives of the very large American investment banks. In the Reformist tradition of keeping the meeting short, a unanimous agreement to loosen bank regulation, reached within 55 minutes by the SEC commissioners, would allegedly cost the world trillions dollars four years later. The commissioners had assumed, it would appear, that the banks would regulate themselves. Their decision allowed the banks to free up capital from their reserves to invest in securitised, high risk 'Mortgage Backed Securities:' the five banks had requested exemption from limits to the amount of debt they could assume imposed by "*old*" regulations: in fact the regulations dated from 1997.[79]

---

[77] "We remain utterly committed to our regulatory mission, but we should be also committed to doing no unnecessary harm or restriction to innovation in the *(financial)* industry and markets." *Mary Schapiro, National Association of Securities Dealers 2006 (quoted in The Wall Street Journal January 16th 2009; italics are mine)*

[78] "NINJA" lending: "No Income; No Job or Assets."

[79] To a European, the regulations may not have seemed that old: perhaps they meant "old" because such rules have been applied as time honoured good practice in banking possibly since the city states of Venice and Genoa developed their banking sectors in the thirteenth century! (*But*, "History is "Bunk."- *Henry Ford*)

One commissioner, who it was said had worked on the 2002 Sarbanes Oxley measures following the corporate accounting problems at ENRON, is quoted in the article as saying that, *"if anything goes wrong, it's going to be an awfully big mess!"* On that count, how right this person had been! They were also warned by an information-systems specialist about the impossibility of managing 'stochastic' risk by the banks' computer models: such models had not protected the stock market from catastrophe in October 1987 and had not prevented the ruinous crash of LTC in 1998.

The "awfully big mess" began when venerable Bear Stearns' agonised with a leverage of 33 to 1, (that is to say that it had $33 of debt for every $1 of capital,) and then Lehmann Brothers went under during the September 2008 liquidity crisis. The leverage crisis at Bear Stearns and winding up Lehman Brothers brought the entire international financial world to a full-blown interbank liquidity crisis, showing at that moment that the US Government did not espouse 'socialist' tactics of bailing out overstuffed, greedy banks; from that point, the crisis became global; like a house of cards, banks worldwide, bloated with bad debt, began to tumble as liquidity dried up.

The fact that REFREP commissioners threw centuries old net capital requirements to the wind and opted for self regulation by the banks despite professional advice to the contrary illustrates not only a dysfunctional Reformist face of the acceptability of riches but also possibly the same kind of unregulated, pioneering, individualistic freedom that allows people to keep guns at home; the protection of such freedoms supports an enterprising and creative state, but it can also be dangerous if it gets out of hand; it allows the murder of some and the ruin of others. *Dysfunctional* Reformism does not oppose financial greed, and *dysfunctional* Republicanism supports considerable personal freedom.

The aggressively forward looking ideal that regards history as "Bunk" illustrates a possible lack of desire to learn from past mistakes. Had the SEC commissioners remembered the collapse of LTC or the stock-market crash of October 1987, or thought about why the Sarbanes Oxley measures had been imposed at all, then they might never have taken the risk of accepting any deregulation at all. Interestingly enough, the SEC had negotiated a right of audit in return for the deregulation decision at the 55 minute meeting, but it would appear that this right had *never* been used up to the time of the first major bank crashes.

American allergy to anything socialist hails back to the days of Senator McArthy's assault on the American left during the Cold War in the 1950s. As a Republican, (in the sense of the Grand Old Party,) McArthy demonised the left wing for generations of Americans: more than half a century later, politicians preferred to kick out bank-rescue plans from Congress and take the risk of a global credit crisis, than to risk taking a decision that could be perceived by American voters as 'socialist.'

The events of 1968, which occurred both in the REFREP and the ROMREP countries of the West had shown, however, that the McArthy brand of 'anti-Socialism' was on the wane. In 1968, the republican young took to the streets in revolution against the established order; events in France and in the United States that year were traumatic: in May 1968 a general strike in France and a left-wing shake up of 'old society' by the largest communist trades union and the French Communist Party almost led to the collapse of the country; in the United States, university students were killed during civil rights movements, and both Martin Luther King and Bobby Kennedy were shot within a few months of each other. Republican Germany suffered from the occupation of factories, and, in Italy, university students stoned each other on campuses across the political divide. Within a few short years urban terrorists appeared as Red Brigades in ROMREP Italy, the Baader-Meinhoff Gang in ROMREP Germany and Action Directe in ROMREP France: their activities included kidnapping and murdering conservative politicians and corporate executives; conversely, the American REFREP young chose the role of free-loving, long haired, pot smoking Hippies in the tradition of the 1968 anti Vietnam-War musical, 'Hair.'

The European monarchies experienced relatively less internal disturbance except "Bobbies" hats being knocked off their heads in Grosvenor Square and lively university debates.

"I'll be nice to him just so long as he doesn't trap me in a corner over Vietnam."

The events of 1968 occurred at the time of Cold War between the Soviet Union and the West: an ideal of 'Eurocommunism' had burgeoned; the Prague Springtime was warming up frosty Czechoslovakia and influencing Western European 'socially involved' students with a desire for revolution. All these events occurred only three years after the close of Vatican II, which had 'updated' Catholicism with ideas such as liberation theology, social responsibility and Kantian freedom of conscience; the events also followed the 1966 destruction of the Palestinian West Bank and happened at a time of widely publicised misery of Palestinian refugees in the Lebanese camps of Sabra and Shatilla. 1968 followed on the heels of France's painful Algerian war and the equally traumatic sequel for American youth to France's colonial adventures in "Indo-China."

In this international chaos, was it any wonder that young ROMREP and REFREP citizens, were they French or American, did not appear to be particularly enthusiastic about the political management of the elder generation? Republicans seemed to be sending their young men to fight foreign wars for barely democratic motives, such as opposing Soviet colonialism. Young people seemed to have difficulty in recognising where the 'right thing to do' lay in killing oriental communists and their women and children in their home country; if they were going to die in a foreign war, they searched, not always successfully, for a clear understanding of why they were risking their young lives. Not all young republicans in 1968 necessarily demonised Communism, whilst others viewed the heady Prague Springtime with the same anticipation and joy that they were to view the extraordinary fall of the Berlin Wall in November 1989.

The established order had 'taken on water;' traditional libertarian republicanism appeared to be sinking; republics were wearing false noses; they had become aggressors in the name of colonialism, and their values appeared to be more despotic and imperialistic, that is to say *more monarchical, than republican* or humanistic. Attacking Communism was claimed to be the 'right thing to do,' because it was claimed to threaten religion and individual freedom, but those who admired Marx and Engels recognised virtue in their humanistic principles that extended even beyond republicanism. Is it any surprise that the ROMREP generation of 1968 remains reputedly, to this day, predominantly left wing, liberal and pacifist?

Whilst the European young of the left took to waving the 'Little Red Book' published by Chairman Mao Tse Tung in preparation for China's Cultural Revolution; the dysfunctionally Reformist *right thing to do* was so poorly accepted by American youth that they demonstrated in the campuses, some to their death: Country

Joe and the Fish caught the flavour when they sang to the immense crowd at Woodstock in the summer of 1969.[80]

In 1968, the republican politicians of the West, both in ROMREP and in REFREP countries, had embroiled themselves in colonial adventures that smacked of imperialism; they had taken to wearing imperial crowns and to xenophobia, bringing war to other republican shores twenty years after European despotism had sacrificed millions of their forebears. Colonialism, Imperialism, xenophobia, foreign war and despotism are all monarchical ideals, and not republican; they are probably, in republican eyes, dysfunctional too.

The lesson that the young of 1968 attempted to teach was in coherence with the principles of the Republic, to restrain the political hand that sends millions of youths to their death in foreign wars; but the lesson was only partially learnt by the leadership; instead of stopping aggression altogether, foreign military adventure just became progressively less costly in young lives, but more costly in materiel and potentially far more destructive of indigenous civilian populations.

---

[80] And it's one, two, three,
What are we fighting for ?
Don't ask me, I don't give a damn,
Next stop is Vietnam;
And it's five, six, seven,
Open up the pearly gates,
Well there ain't no time to wonder why,
Whoopee! we're all gonna die.

© *Country Joe & the Fish*
Chorus from: "I-Feel-Like-I'm-Fixin'-To-Die Rag" sung at Woodstock in the summer of 1969 (to a background chorus of "Wackadoo..Wackadoo...") The origin of the band's name comes from Mao Tse Tung's's saying about "the fish who swim in the sea of the people;" the Country Joe part refers to Joseph Stalin, whose nickname during World War II was "Country Joe."

CHAPTER 9

INTERACTIONS AND CONTRASTS

REFMON and ROMREP

The Grid is a practical tool in the office: it could help to choose, for example, which person to send to negotiate an international contract with a Russian: would I send an Englishman or a Frenchman? I may reason as above that the Russian has REPublican political leanings, and, as an Orthodox Christian, may see the world through ROManist-type eyes: so, if I expect his behaviour to be closer to that of a ROMREP, I might prefer to send a Frenchman, a Portuguese, an Austrian or an Italian, who are also ROMREPs, rather than an Englishman, who is a REFMON; I may not send an Englishman if I have an equally capable Frenchman, because, while opposing cultures may sometimes attract, cultural *differences* have the potential to destroy.

During the Cold War, who in Europe, if not the REFMON Brits, fostered Cold War hostility with the ROMREP Russians? Was a "Kim" caricature of the patrician, Oxbridge educated, gentleman spy more likely to have evoked warm, fuzzy feelings of friendship in the bowels of a third generation Ukrainian Party member of peasant stock than a "Klaus" caricature of a hard drinking, be-whiskered Austrian in a feathered hat and one foot in his mountain farm? Probably not! The ROMREP Austrians had functioning frontier posts with the Soviet Union during the Cold War; for decades Vienna was the portal of business with the Soviets.

The French and Italian Communist Parties grew to enormous proportions by sending many for training to 'Mother' Russia during the Cold War, but not the British! When the Georgian conflict with Russia flared in 2008, who but French President, Nicholas Sarkozy, found sufficient common ground to talk to Dimitri Medvedev in the seeming absence of any American reaction whatever? Which cultures have integrated well into France, if not the Portuguese, who are ROMREPs too? If I were to advise a ROMREP Frenchman where to send his son to learn English, I would advise ROMREP Ireland, and for a holiday, ROMREP Italy or ROMREP Portugal!

Do the British feel comfortable among the Dutch or the Scandinavians? Yes, they do: the Dutch are REFMONs too, as are the Danish, Norwegians and Swedes.

In a restaurant in the South of France one evening in the summer of 2008, we sat next to a table of Australian tourists: a pretty young French girl with a smattering of broken English was serving their table. The loudest Australian fellow, there for a bit of fun, said, "Hello, darling: *you're looking beautiful* tonight!" My wife and I watched as the girl's eyes lit up; she smiled at the Australian for the rest of the evening, giving him such good service that we had to remind her from time to time that we needed to be served too. While she was at another table, the Australians got up and walked out without even leaving a tip. Her face fell when she returned to their empty table; the sadness that darkened her smile was genuinely poignant.

The Australian, technically a REFMON,[81] in the informal manner of his countrymen, had made a meaningless (for him) comment very probably in kindness to a young ROMREP woman: she, not knowing how 'direct' Australians can be, had taken the compliment as a ROMREP woman might, *seriously*, and had responded enthusiastically, expecting, no doubt, another approach from this young man; *he*, on the other hand, had not accounted for

---

[81] the Australian head of state is Her Majesty, Queen Elizabeth II

the fact that Romanist, elliptical thought makes such a serious event as flirting long and complex; when a Frenchman courts, he builds the relationship step by careful step, just as the Victorians used to. The Australian's compliment would have won a laugh from a Finnish, or even from a British, woman (REFREP and REFMON,) who would never have taken him seriously, but, for this young French girl, the compliment 'delivered at Mach 3.0' swept her so much off her feet, that the episode ended in frustration.

The work of K. Lewin in 'Topological Psychology' (1936) gives a complementary view of this exchange by applying his theory of 'Specific' and 'Diffuse' relationships: the Specific relationship is, for example, that existing between REFREPs, where the personal and private inner space of each individual is *not* exposed in normal communication or is only exposed as a small *relevant* sector; the Diffuse relationship is that existing between ROMREPS, where the personal and private inner space must be exposed across all its various aspects before communication can function. The Australian no doubt thought, because no one could seriously expect to be admitted to his private space, that his 'friendly' comment would not lead to the expectation of any further contact: he was wrong; the French girl, who would expect only after some time to enter into any young man's private space and who would take such entry as an open door to the rest of his inner space, was left breathless with anticipation.

It is a similar reaction that many Europeans have to the American statement made with a friendly smile, "Gimme a call, *sometime*." The American says this without really meaning it; the European may take the request seriously and shocks the American when he really does make the call.[82] These are minor events; the French

---

[82] When Americans "let in" a German, French or Italian colleague into one compartment of their public space and show their customary openness and friendliness, that person may assume that they have been admitted to diffuse private space. They may expect the American to show equivalent friendship in all life spaces and be offended if he or she comes to their town without contacting them.
Trompenaars & Hampden-Turner; Riding the Waves of Culture

girl will get over it, although it may affect the way she thinks about Australians for the rest of her life; the real problem is that *the consequences of similar misunderstanding in times of international crisis can be catastrophic!*

Do we not marvel at how the European Economic Community survives the chronic difficulties of communication between individuals of different cultures? In September 2008, I was intrigued to be invited a day's European wide conference organised by the Association of French Expatriates at the Quai d'Orsay in Paris, where the French Ministry of Foreign Affairs is located in a magnificent period building overlooking the Seine river. The event coincided with the six-month French presidency of the European Union, and took as its theme improving the life of expatriate Europeans within the EEC, with introductory papers outlining themes such as healthcare, justice and pensions. About 200 delegates appeared from 24 of the 27 countries of the Union. The smallest delegation was the German (REFREP) one with only 2 members and the largest outside the French (ROMREP) group was the Italian (ROMREP, too) one with about 20 members.

The context within which this meeting was held had seemed clear enough for the British delegation to draw up a page of seven short sentences the previous day summarising their wishes in the areas to be discussed, including, for example, expatriate voting rights. The wish list was printed and distributed to all the delegates by the French organisers at the start of the meeting: within the hour, the organisers distributed a new draft paper called the "Paris Declaration," a document of six pages which had already been modified to include almost the entire British wish list in various positions in the text. The British delegation was delighted, and its members read on as the speeches and round tables continued, as various position statements were read from the floor and such questions as double nationality and divorce laws were discussed. Then the delegates noticed that ratifying the Lisbon Treaty had somehow insidiously become the speakers' priority issue; as the various French Members of the European Parliament and

Senators took the microphone; it became virtually the only issue they spoke of; and then a French Government Minister spoke about creating a "Social Europe."

As much as the expatriate agenda had been presented in good faith by the organisers, suspicion grew among the delegates that they had been ambushed, because a parallel agenda had been introduced by the speakers; of course there had been no problem in adding the British wish list, because the thrust of the document, which all were expected to sign at the end of the day, incorporated an unobtrusive item or two: that of supporting a treaty that had been voted out by the Irish Republican voters using their veto power, and that of supporting the deployment of a model of social responsibility within a community of 27 countries that were not all necessarily in agreement on one single way to legislate for national labour.

A little background to Franco-British schizophrenia over the EEC could be useful: the European Common Market had been set up in Grandfather's time, (the Treaty of Rome dates from 1957,) to calm the waters between France and Germany under the pretext of common coal and steel, and agricultural, policies. The British were kept out until 1973, when they joined an organisation called the European *Common Market*, under the assumption that creating a wider market for European goods and services would be the right thing to do. The subsequent development was two-brained: on the one side, the British continued to see nothing more than a market of international neighbours for their goods and services; on the other, the French had a ROMREP vision of European *political* union around a *'humanistic,' federalist*, model, which they appeared to take for granted would be *republican*.

Successive British governments pushed to include more and more countries in the European group, and even saw no problem, with encouragement from their American allies, in welcoming Muslim Turkey to a basket of nations, now including ex-Soviet satellites, which, two decades earlier, had been at *Cold* War with the rest of Europe: after all, the EEC was intended to be nothing more than a market place, and a friendly Turkey might be a useful Muslim avenue into the more intimidating Middle East! The French, with their ROMREP idea of Europe, had observed with ever increasing worry the growing mixed bag of nations joining the Union concerned that the group would not only become ungovernable, but end up such a dog's breakfast that any notion of political union would become laughable. They took things in hand and made a first attempt at defending their vision of political union by launching a document entitled, 'The Convention,' written by ex-President Valéry Giscard d'Estaing: in plain vanilla language it made an attempt to *codify* a constitutional base to the ever growing and increasingly ungovernable group of nations. Unfortunately, the nature of the document required citizens to vote the measure in referenda throughout the EEC including France; after a number of favourable votes in other countries, the French, to general surprise, voted Giscard's project out!

The constitutional project was rehashed shortly afterwards at a meeting of EEC ministers in Lisbon and 'force marched' into 27 political agendas because, renamed as a *Treaty*, it ostensibly avoided the need for any more referenda being voted out by ill informed citizens voting on the basis of misunderstood issues. The Treaty seemed a foregone conclusion until plucky Ireland stood its ground and claimed that the Irish would not permit such a Treaty to be applied without a national vote; so they voted, and used their veto too to vote the Lisbon Treaty out just as the French had voted out the Convention; Ireland looked like a sturdy Celt resisting the Roman armies; an image close to the heart of any fan of the *French* comic strip, Asterix! The Irish position had been understandable in view of the day's speakers' comments about having to be "*lucid* about the *obstacles* to the treaty" (sic) and that "Subsidiarity *implies* Proportionality" (sic): this implied that the main sticking point for the Irish would be that the treaty implied the loss of veto power that even small countries currently held in the Community on issues of national constitutional consequence: each member state in the Treaty of Lisbon would have to accept majority decisions; in fifty or so policy areas, countries would lose their power to refuse to honour Community decisions because they would have to abide by 'Qualified Majority Voting,' which would replace unanimity rule: this would set smaller countries such as Ireland with their reduced 'clout' at a potential disadvantage in the Community.

The question of applying the French social model to other countries in Europe had become thorny since the French socialists had launched a 'humanistic' 35 hour working week in 2000, making France structurally uncompetitive at a time when the Chinese labour hour was one fifteenth of the cost of the French labour hour: France had already lost in excess of three million jobs from its industrial sector over the preceding three decades, almost all of it to foreign competition, including China's; the outcome was predictably catastrophic for chronically overstretched French unemployment; in the meanwhile, the Germans, already with twice France's industrial economic weight, were going the opposite way and *lengthening* the working week to safeguard Germany's international competitiveness. Observers asked Europe-wide, "How can you work less and earn more?" The French replied elliptically that their economy benefits from a "French Exception," but to give credit to M. Sarkozy's new government a pragmatic move was afoot in late 2008 to scrap the 35 hour week.

So, at the Quai d'Orsay, the British delegation found on the one hand its Irish neighbour under pressure to revote, but this time, so to speak, "*properly*!" and, on the other, that France's international neighbours were being encouraged to follow a 'social' model that wasn't theirs, and worse, did not appear to work. The meeting had been called for a completely different motive, and a document would be signed at the end of the day, implicitly signifying agreement of the British delegation! Was this really a surprise? After all, Jean-Jacques Rousseau had forewarned in 'The Social Contract,' "*...whoever refuses to obey the general will shall be constrained to do so by the whole body, which means nothing other than that he shall be forced to be free...*"

During the discussions the questions flew: the British delegation asked for more simplicity and modesty to be introduced into the Paris Declaration and suggested concentrating more on changing *means* to obtain the ends rather than on assumptions about humanistic social models; also, was it necessary to put it all in writing? A Belgian delegate stood and said a few sharp words about the "English" position, which was met with British phlegm and cheers from the 20 strong Italian delegation.

A British representative then told the Government Minister that, as France was leading the world on the values of *'equality* and of *fraternity,'* it seemed strange that France didn't also defend the *liberty* of other EEC nations to do as they pleased in setting their own working hours; the minister replied to the effect that France could not accept the idea of EEC countries being able to compete with each other on the basis of labour cost; an unsurprising comment at a time the French were possibly working the shortest working week in Europe.

So the day continued to its completion of a compromise document that was signed, but not by all; that was important to the delegates in the room, but of questionable weight in Brussels, but that was in writing; its thrust implicitly supported a political model and got the plug in about the Lisbon Treaty. A few months later, the Sarkozy government, with France coming to the end of its six month presidency of the European Union, triumphantly announced the Irish Republic's decision to vote again on the Lisbon Treaty. Perhaps the British delegation should not have been so surprised; both France and the Irish Republic are ROMREP nations. When this book went to press, Europe was waiting the outcome of the Irish vote with baited breath.

Introducing a document incorporating themes that were foreign to the primary objective led the delegates to feel that they had been ambushed, showing that even republican diplomacy can follow Machiavellian lines. The British delegation had managed a coup in getting its own declaration published; because monarchists know their Machiavelli as well as anyone!

The fact that Britain is an island monarchy lies at the heart of the conflict of views between ROMREP France and the REFMON United Kingdom: Machiavelli stated that a prince does not do well to trust foreign neighbours, who are likely to make a bid for the loyalties of his subjects; France was seen as attempting to create an overarching federalism in Europe that would severely hamper the freedom of the British to be masters in their own island, and that would give new impetus to republicanism and to humanism in a monarchy that traditionally has no great taste for either; if the British have not joined the Euro and maintained their Sterling independence for the time being, it is to protect the Bank of England's prerogative to manipulate its currency as it sees fit and not as 'foreigners' in a European Central Bank might do; this is classical Machiavellian, monarchical distrust of international neighbours.

The fact that a nation votes out a new constitution for the EEC, and then criticises another for doing the same thing, seems to reconcile yes with no and to be classically elliptical; having the word "Liberty" in a national motto and then appearing to refuse it to other nations, who wish to have their own labour law respected, or who *also* wish to vote 'no' in a referendum, seems elliptical; there may be British misunderstanding of the French use of the word, which is intended to signify protection of the collective from arbitrary rule of the individual; again, in a discussion on the difficulty of harmonising the divorce laws during the conference, ROMREP delegates of a Roman Catholic nation, who know that the Vatican is at fundamental odds with the principle itself of divorce, supported the notion of facilitating divorce under a single Europe-wide law: this was in line with Voltaire's primitive anti-Christianity, and dysfunctionally Romanist, and elliptical too.

Romanist work is about humanism, that is to say about employment, and not about 'capitalistic' profit: the outcome of a Europe-wide, short working week to avoid labour competition between European nations in complete disregard of global competition from high-growth, low labour-cost nations would be in diametric opposition to the Protestant Work Ethic of numerous other Northern European states in the Community. Was it just a coincidence that Europe's largest country, Germany, had sent only two delegates to the conference? I had attended a conference in 2007, where a French-speaking, German diplomat had criticised France's efforts to impose its own administrative models on the workings of the European Community, and this event may have to lent some weight to his opinion.

The 'humanistic' model was preached under an assumption of modernism and of moral probity uncomfortably akin to the Reformist ideal of it being unquestionably the 'right thing to do:' this behaviour convinced me that dysfunctional Reformism and dysfunctional Republicanism may well share a taste for moral universalism; the text of the Paris Declaration, for example, speaks extensively of the rights of *citizens*; the word *"subjects"* is never used despite Europe's twelve monarchies and principalities.[83]

When the British delegation asked what had been intended as a simple question, "In the name of which *morality* are you proposing these ideas?" it was met with horror; it had probably not occurred to many ROMREP delegates that there could be any 'morality' other than that of republican humanism.

Fons Trompenaars' and Charles Hampden-Turner's book, 'Riding the Waves of Culture,' brings further light onto that day's social dynamics by giving the following handy advice: if a Universalist, (who exhibits rule-based behaviour, such as a REFMON,) is dealing with a Particularist, (who shows relationship centred

---

[83] I later learnt from the British Consul General in Paris that the British Nationality Law passed in 1981 confines the status of British *Subject* to certain Indians who had a former connection with British India and those in the Republic of Ireland who had declared their intention before 1949 of keeping British nationality. Otherwise, the vast majority of residents are correctly now called British *citizens*. The act was passed it seems to allow the Crown to stop recognising Commonwealth citizens of other states as British subjects, but the majority of categories of nationality that now exist in the Law only appear to talk of the status of *citizenship* in Britain. Was the baby not thrown out with the bath water? Does this not still conceivably leave 11 other states in Europe that have subjects rather than citizens?

behaviour, such as a ROMREP,) he needs to *focus more on relationships than on rules; to expect contractual arrangements to be questioned and to be modified; to build trust by honouring the change in mutual balance; to expect that each participant will hold his own unique perspective on reality, and to expect relationships to change.* The advice given to the Particularist in dealing with a Universalist is to *focus more on rules than on relationships; to expect difficulty in changing already agreed contractual arrangements; to build trust around honouring one's word or contract; to expect that the only truth is that which has already been agreed to, and to accept that a deal is a deal!* [84]

A British friend of mine; I will call him, Michael; succeeded in getting a posting to the United States with the International French company he was working for. After three very successful years over there, and following ten years of career with the Group, the C.E.O. invited him back to Paris to offer him the position of Managing Director of one of the French subsidiaries. Michael accepted the job with a handshake and returned to prepare his transfer and that of his family to Paris. This Group C.E.O. had given his word, and, after his posting, Michael imagined that the C.E.O. was duty-bound to keep it, because where Michael had just spent three years, that was the 'right thing to do.'

When he turned up at the offices of the subsidiary he was due to manage, the Chairman, a Frenchman close to retirement, and with very little international experience, asked him first to accept Board responsibility for Marketing and Development; this was intended to be just for a few months so that he could 'learn the ropes.' Expecting the elder to keep his word, as one would in REFREP society, Michael agreed.

After six months, Michael was still not in the job he had been promised, and his concern grew day-by-day. A French Board colleague, let's call him Bernard, who had been many years in the

---

[84] Universalism and Particularism as behavioural models had previously been introduced through Parsons' work in 1951, "The Social System," see Appendix C.

company, and who knew the Chairman very well, kept on reporting back to Michael that he was getting continual visits from Michael's staff with complaints about how difficult it was to work for him. Michael was surprised: Marketing and Development were going well; he was already launching new product lines; and a new three-year plan at last gave some visibility to new product development. Michael was professionally concerned with time; time was money.

After nine months, the Chairman informed Michael that he had chosen to put Bernard in the job of Managing Director, but that Michael could keep the marketing job if he wished. Michael complained and confronted the Chairman at a disastrous meeting with the Group C.E.O., who had 'promised' him the job in the first place; however the Group C.E.O. supported the decision of the Division Chairman against Michael's complaint.

What had happened to cause such catastrophic failure in Michael's career? Leaving aside the obvious rivalry between Bernard and Michael, and, as it was later found out, Bernard's influence both over the Chairman, and Michael's subordinates, an analysis of Michael's REFMON behaviour modified by his three years of REFREP experience give behavioural pointers.

As a REFMON, Michael's basic management style was frankly 'one on one;' as a Universalist, and hence mistrustful of a French boss who was not immediately keeping his word of giving him the promised position, Michael's cultural tendency towards isolation took the upper hand in the early months; as a REFMON he became secretive and seemed to remain relatively aloof from his colleagues, showing little emotion concerning the downturn in his career; he continued to do what *he* thought was a good job, directing his team in effective action and ensuring that deadlines were being met, possibly giving rather more weight to time than to building relationships.

Both above and below him in the hierarchy, he was sandwiched by ROMREPs: his subordinates functioned in an egalitarian, information-sharing and informal environment; they looked upon their bosses with the child dependence of the ROMREP, and expected Michael less to set long-term goals and vision, than to spend time in relationship building; they expected discussion and debate to ensure their buy-in to Michael's vision and a fraternal ear to listen to their complaints.

Michael later claimed to me that working in the United States had been so much easier for him because his subordinates there needed only to understand their instructions, and did not necessarily wish to spend time on understanding background or why the instructions had been given at all; meetings had been faster and more effective because he could tell his staff what he wanted, answer questions and be quickly out of the meeting room to get on with the rest of his work; he had felt no need or desire at all to spend time 'speaking to the inner space' of his subordinates: the Americans seemed to function happily that way, but the French killed his career for it.

He had been shocked by the length of time after arriving in France, not only that his subordinates were asking of him, but also that Management-Board meetings were taking; these were run by the Chairman, who would start the meetings at 5:00pm every Monday evening, and cheerfully go on to 9:30 pm; Michael was all the more concerned that discussion seemed to go round and round in circles; it rarely seemed to go anywhere, and decisions seemed to be only very rarely taken, although, with all the Cartesian discussion of 'ins and outs,' he admitted they were invariably good decisions and not just inductively, pragmatically 'at least half right.'[85]

After a few years, Michael left the group, and embarked upon a new career. He had learned a bitter lesson: working with the French team, he now believes he should have better shared

---

[85] "You can always count on the Americans to do the right thing – after they've tried everything else."
Winston Churchill

information; he ought to have responded to the childlike dependence of his subordinates as a reassuring father figure, taking the time to talk, to discuss and to debate his points of view until he was sure that they had bought in, even if the time necessary to do this appeared to be ridiculously excessive; he should have taken the time with his people that the Chairman was taking with his own Management Board, just talking round and round issues. His line of behaviour should have been to focus primarily on relationships rather than on deadlines; to forget rules, and to expect agreements and relationships to evolve; he should have been more sensitive to change in his boss's positions and possibly have reacted more energetically; he should have searched to understand and to honour the opinions of others. He should have appeared less aloof and distant, fraternally sharing information about his worries; had he shown perhaps more of the emotion he had felt following the disappointment of not getting the position, the reaction of his senior management might have been more sympathetic: his phlegm concerning his obvious career problem was not culturally in line with the classic Gallic outburst[86] that would have been expected. On his return from the United States, Michael was in a serious cultural mismatch with the French company he had been invited to manage.

The picture is even bleaker on the corporate side: the management decision to invite Michael to take the job should have been respected; the fact that it wasn't, discredited the 10 years of successful track record he had already shown with the company: competent senior international managers ought to know that cultural adjustments always occur with international moves and that they always take time. The fact that the Group C.E.O. gave away to the politics of his subordinate, the subsidiary Chairman, and did not keep his word with Michael, shows well the fickleness of Particularism: seen through the eyes of the Universalist, his decision was not the right one: the Group C.E.O. was rightly or wrongly more concerned with relationships than with any rule-based behaviour such as keeping his word; it

---

[86] "Coup de gueule." *Untranslatable*

seemed to him no doubt normal that his contract with Michael could be questioned and modified; for him, there was *no* deal; changes in mutual balance would have to be accounted for; the Particularist *expects* relations to change.

Had Michael just returned from Britain instead of from the United States, he might have been a little more Machiavellian and circumspect before accepting the job; he might have thrashed out safer rules of engagement at the outset. Had the Group C.E.O. been an American, Michael would have got the job anyway; the question then would have been how long he would be able to hold it down without having a Gallic mutiny on his hands.

REFREP and ROMMON

To avoid cultural mistakes, we need to recognise what different cultures have to argue about or to agree on. Would a Spanish national manager of an American subsidiary in Spain be that enthusiastic about receiving a delegation from his head office insisting that its visiting members should meet him not alone, *but in the presence of his whole team*? This is a very American thing to do: it may not worry another American, so would anyone in the delegation give a second thought to the fact that the Spaniard is a ROMMON, who believes in hierarchy, personal service to his boss, and confidentiality, not to mention that monarchical class consciousness probably brings him to believe that he is somehow different from his subordinates? Not only would the Spaniard have to get over the insult of not being seen alone, or, at least, first, but he would also have to make a paradigm shift to work with the team when his style is probably quite "top-down" and "one-on-one;" even his subordinates would be surprised to participate in a meeting that 'belongs' to their boss; they might even feel threatened by it or outraged that their boss should have been insulted so; they might conclude that such lack of confidence means he is about to be fired. It's probable that the Americans would crease up laughing in disbelief that such *'anachronistic'* behaviour *still* exists, but it is a natural consequence of monarchical values; they may laugh for similar reasons and fail to notice the scowl on the face of a tribal Muslim Afghan, or of a Saudi, or of an Indo-European, such as an Iranian or a Turk, all who *arguably* exhibit equivalent ROMMON-*type* behaviour: then one day they might find themselves the subject of hostility, or of an inexplicable terrorist outrage, or of war in a distant land. Even the task oriented matrix structures in industry, which are prevalent and function well in the United States, challenge a Spaniard's ideal of loyalty to his boss: bosses are like fathers, you can't have two of them.

Many aspects of American business culture, which is generally thought to be best practice worldwide, pose difficulty for those who are not REFREPs: for example, business education regards emotionally detached rationality as scientifically necessary; whereas, ROMREPs and ROMMONs regard such neutrality as emotionally 'dead,' and think that hiding feelings is a mark of deceit; as a result, the Americans are reputed to view the French, Italians or Spanish as flamboyant, hierarchical and emotional, whereas the French, Italians or Spanish may well view the Americans as aggressive and thoughtless.

Feedback meetings to explore mistakes are viewed by REFREP Americans as efficient and unthreatening, whereas the pluralistic German, with his complex cultural mix, which may even include nostalgic Monarchism and dysfunctional Romanism, could well view one as a forum for enforced admission of error, with serious consequences for any continuing trust between international managers.

ROMANIST AND REFORMIST

The book, 'Riding the Waves of Culture,' describes the results of a survey on the concept of *freedom*: on the one hand persons were asked whether they agree with (a) the ideal of *individual freedom* and opportunity to develop themselves, or on the other hand with (b) the importance of continuously taking care of their fellow human *beings even if it obstructs individual freedom and development*. Respondents from ROMREP France, Portugal and

Italy tended to choose (b) whereas respondents from the REFMON United Kingdom and Netherlands as well as REFREP Switzerland and United States tended to choose (a.) In these replies, the approach of the Romanist to the welfare of the poor, so different from that of the suspicious Reformist, isolating himself from the beggar, stands out in the answers given; the ideal of American republican liberty is construed to allow a maximum of personal freedom to the individual, very much in the spirit of the pioneer, which lends such an image of vitality to the American way of life. The republican ideal of liberty construed by the French is altogether different and stands out in contrast: theirs is not an ideal of individual pioneering freedom at all, but that of the collective freedom from the arbitrary power of an individual or of a group of individuals which so often seems to polarise sections of the citizenry against its government.

Was it any surprise that ROMREP French President Sarkozy visited the REFREP United States following the Subprime crisis to give the Americans lessons on 'financial *moralisation'* (sic)? What other country but France during the nationalisation of Freddie Mac and Fannie May debt in late 2008 would have done so? Within a few weeks, M. Sarkozy had united most of the European Union countries around a bail-out plan, which included virtual nationalisation of the bigger, illiquid banks; the plan reversed bank privatisation decisions that had allowed France to climb out of decades of socialist policy; at the same time radio broadcasts in the country crowed about the unacceptable face of Capitalism, and asked whether American influence on the world stage was not weakening. Could the Subprime crisis have occurred first in a ROMMON country, for example? I think not: the Romanist is suspicious of lucre, and Machiavelli is forever reminding his Prince to be prudent, and *high risk is not compatible with survival*. The shakiness of Northern Rock in the United Kingdom showed, however, that such an event appeared perfectly likely to occur in a REFMON community; the Subprime crisis might thus appear to be linked, between the REFREP United States and the REFLMON United Kingdom, with dysfunctional Reformism.

Possibly the most perceptive description of the difference between the liberty of the French Revolution and that of American individualism was given by Abraham Lincoln in a speech he gave in Baltimore in 1864, where he compared freedom from the yoke of bondage with the individual freedom of the pioneer; admittedly his theme concerned the cleavage between the Union and the Confederacy, but his words are no less relevant to the difference between ROMREP and REFREP societies today, not only in the field of domestic policy, but more critically, in the one of international relations.

"The shepherd drives the wolf from the sheep's throat, for which the sheep thanks the shepherd as a liberator, while the wolf denounces him for the same act as the destroyer of liberty.... Plainly the sheep and the wolf are not agreed upon a definition of the word liberty; and precisely the same difference prevails to-day among us human creatures, even in the North, and all professing to love liberty. Hence we behold the processes by which thousands are daily passing from under the yoke of bondage, hailed by some as the advance of liberty, and bewailed by others as the destruction of all liberty."

REPUBLICAN AND MONARCHICAL

In the same issue of the International Herald Tribune quoted on page 130, it was reported that a coded diplomatic message concerning the reported conversation of a British diplomat in Afghanistan had been leaked to a French satirical newspaper; French diplomats had qualified the leak as a "diplomatic disaster." The British diplomat, who was reported to have said that he thought an *acceptable dictator* to be the best solution for the future of Afghanistan, had allegedly added that foreign military presence in the country was "part of the problem."

It is understandable that French and American Republicans would be scandalised by the idea of putting a country into the hands of a dictator, (acceptable or not:) on the one hand Rousseau's diatribes against feudal monarchy preclude any idea of putting any form of personal arbitrary rule at the head of any country, tyrannical or not, and, on the other hand, American Reformists would have tortured themselves with the thought that this is just not the *right thing to do*. The French diplomats were all the more embarrassed that France had just sent in 700 more troops to join the ones already being "part of the problem;" and 1968 had painfully shown how young French republicans take to far flung invasion for obscure, and, possibly, imperialist, motives.

The British diplomat's words, if they were correctly reported, may well have been made in *irony* and with Anglo-Saxon *phlegm*: the British may indeed view the idea of placing a tribal feudal chief in control of this 'awful mess' with the superior equanimity of monarchists, especially if a pragmatic solution avoided perpetuating the war against the Taliban and stopped the slaughter of more innocents: Saddam Hussein had already shown the tyrant's efficiency in attaining stability in Iraq a few decades earlier; unfortunately he had slaughtered innocents too; but is it surprising that the arbitrary power and privilege of tough dictatorship seen through monarchical eyes would not appear to carry the stigma it does when seen through republican ones? Is such rule, after all, so very far removed from monarchy's own distant feudal origins? One might almost think so; but one would have to forget the vigorous, isolated British opposition to Hitler and to Mussolini, at least from 1939.

GLOSSARY

Aggregation
From the Latin word, *aggregare*, which means to 'herd together,' aggregation, is the tendency in certain societies to give priority to collective ideals over individualistic ones.

Asceticism
Asceticism is the practice of self discipline and the systematic avoidance of sensory pleasure or luxury.

Calvinism
A protestant theology, which advocates asceticism and is based on Jean Calvin's (1509-1564) *Deterministic* conclusion that, if God is indeed all knowing (omniscient) and all powerful (omnipotent,) then, from all eternity, He necessarily has predestined every individual either to salvation or to damnation. The individual cannot, then, do anything to influence his own destiny as either a condemned sinner or as a 'worldly saint.' The human philosophical rigour of Determinism gives Calvinist doctrine a reputation for being 'this-worldly,' that is to say not in any sense mystic.

Cartesianism
This is the mode of thought of the French philosopher, René Descartes, the author of the phrase, "Cogito, ergo sum," (I am thinking, therefore I exist.) Descartes attempted to construct a corpus of philosophy based on scepticism, this is to say by putting all premises in doubt, and then as a logician by progressing purely on the basis of deductive logic. His philosophy nonetheless assumed two important premises at the foundation of its structure: "I am thinking, therefore I exist," and "God exists."

Catharsis
Catharsis is the flush of pent up feelings triggered by an emotional or a sensory experience.

Censorious isolation
This is the combination of mistrust, prejudice and bigotry resulting in contempt for others and in isolation of the individual from the society of others, particularly not of his social class.

Consequentialism
Consequentialism is the view that ethical rightness is based on the effectiveness of an action in procuring desirable results, otherwise said that, "the end justifies the means."

Deductive logic
Aristotle's original formulation of deductive logic was the use of 'watertight' inference: his construction was, "If A equals B, and x equals A, then x equals B." For example, "If all men are male, and John is a man, then John is a male." The conclusion is entirely, and only, based on the premises, and guaranteed to be true, or 'entailed,' only if the premises are true. (See below: Inductive Logic.)

Deontology
Deontology is a duty- and intention-based ethic that holds that certain actions are either right or wrong irrespective of their consequences.

Determinism
Determinism is the theory that every event has prior cause and that, therefore, any state is a necessary consequence of its previous state. A fully deterministic world contradicts the idea of the free will of its agents.

Dogmatism
Dogmatism is a firm assertion of opinion, including the proclamation of ideas, which are not necessarily in agreement with empirical knowledge, as being true and factual.

Egocentricity
Egocentricity is the tendency for individuals to centre on their own interest rather than on the interest of others, or of society in general; it can be associated with suspicion and mistrust of others and with aggressively self-centred behaviour called 'machismo,' which is strong masculine pride, the word being derived from the Mexican Spanish macho, meaning 'male.'

Elliptic thought; ellipsis
I call the thought process by which people internalise mystical claims on faith alone, "elliptic." Elliptic thought rationalises paradox by making, for example, un-provable ideas, or ones in apparent contradiction with empirical data, credible; elliptical construction leaves uncertainty unsaid, assumes premises on faith alone, and gives equivalent weight to theory and to synthesis as to fact and to evidence; it helps to deduce complexity without proof of essential premises on faith alone; it stems from, and reinforces, the conviction that 'truths' are not plain and simple; it encourages tolerance for argument on more artistic and creative planes than logic, but it provokes a 'flight' to Cartesian scepticism and to deductive logic to compensate the 'strain on the mind.' Pre-Roman literature gives three meanings to the word "elliptic:" *defective* (Theognis; Plato; Lysias; Eustatius); *incomplete* (Plotinus), and *falling short* (Aristophanes; Aristotle; Polybius.) The contemporary sense is: an *incomplete expression*; a phrase *lacking a word or words needed to complete the sense* of the sentence; *leaving something out*; *to be understood*; *intentionally lost* or obfuscated; arriving at a *conclusion without delineating its steps*.

Emotive machismo
This is the combination of dysfunctional 'spoilt-child' behaviour in reaction to strong maternal influence in matriarchal societies, with 'machismo,' which is aggressive masculine pride, the word being derived from the Mexican Spanish *macho*, meaning 'male.'

Empiricism
Empiricism is the use of experience or experimentation to confirm a concept or belief.

Inductive logic
An inductive argument is a general principle inferred or extrapolated from empirical observations. Its conclusion does not follow necessarily from the premises: for example, the premises can be true, but the conclusion false. Inductive thought leads to a probable (i.e. uncertain) conclusion, which is supported, but not entailed (i.e. made certain,) by the premises.
Aristotle propounded inductive logic, which seemed to meet the needs of his biological enquiries, and he accepted premises based on "reputable opinions," which were held by most "clever men." The ultimate source of knowledge, in his view, came from the generalisation of human perception. Plato gave abstract forms the leading role in his ontology and regarded thought, with its deductive power, rather than perception, as the way to understand reality. Aristotle used the idea of 'tradition' in the growth of knowledge, and St Thomas Aquinas's admiration of Aristotelian thought led the Church to include this inductive concept of 'tradition' to substantiate part of its doctrine (see paragraph 82 in the Catechism of the Catholic Church,) but this was only after the Church's initial attempt to suppress Aristotle's writings altogether.

Irony
The use of words to convey a meaning opposite to their literal meaning

Linearity
The application of God-given, human logic to spirituality, refusing all premises which are not strictly biblically based, is termed linear, pragmatic, 'this-worldly' thought, as opposed to dogmatic, elliptic, 'other-worldly' thought. Linear thought tolerates inductive logic well.

Matriarchal society
Society which is inspired by a maternal ethic, containing not only the non-aggressive characteristics of femininity, but also the Freudian idea of the submission of the 'defenceless' infant's will to the 'dominating' power of the nurturing mother.

Monarchism

This is the support of the principle of supreme power held by an unelected individual within a 'feudal' (or, more recently, constitutional) system of rights and duties, which are intended to subordinate individuals to the monarch's will in return for privilege, and to encourage protection of the monarch, of his family and of his possessions.

Moral Absolutism

This is the belief that certain actions are either absolutely right or absolutely wrong no matter what the circumstances or what the outcome.

Numinous

Numinous is a term coined by German theologian Rudolf Otto to describe that which is *wholly other*. It is the *mysterium tremendum et fascinans* that leads to belief in deities, the supernatural, the sacred, the holy, and the transcendent. It can be considered as that "intense feeling of unknowingly knowing that there is something which cannot be seen." Such "knowing" can overcome a person with feelings of awe, as one might feel in a cathedral; next to a silent stream; on a lonely road; early in the morning, or in watching a lovely sunset. The word is equally applied to the sensation of fright experienced in sensing the presence of evil, such as a ghost or an evil spirit. The word was used by Otto in his book *Das Heilige* (1917,) and was an important concept in the writings of Carl Jung and of C. S. Lewis.

Other-worldliness

Other-worldliness is the mystic belief that isolated, ascetic, God-centred behaviour in life can merit favourable placement after death in the 'other world' (i.e. Heaven ;) it implies disinterest in the agent's environment, in nature and in the human condition.

Phlegm

Composure; equanimity; calmness; self composure

Paradox

Paradox is an argument with seemingly unobjectionable premises, which leads by proper inference to a contradictory conclusion.

Particularism

Relationship-centred behaviour.

Pragmatism

Pragmatism is the choice of theories, beliefs, policies and decisions on the basis of their probable success.

Privilege
Privilege is a special right, advantage, or immunity allowed to a particular person or a group, including the right to say or to write something without the risk of punishment by a superior such as the Monarch or the state. Individual privilege can be more or less acceptable according to social paradigms, and typically increases to the benefit of individuals through progressively higher social levels in class systems.

Reformism
Reformism is defined *in this essay* as that body of spiritual ideas that result from ascetic Calvinist Protestantism, and which challenges Roman Catholic doctrine; **Reformists** are those whose behaviour and attitudes, functional or dysfunctional, arise from Calvinist Protestantism, *whether they be of the Calvinist creed or not.* Catholics living in an essentially Reformist state would probably develop a significant proportion of Reformist attitudes over the long term.

Relativism
Relativism is the opinion that ethical rightness or wrongness is determined by culture and traditions.

Republicanism
Republicanism is the political philosophy that the state embodies the supreme power of its citizens through their elected representatives; it opposes the philosophy of individual power, such as that of a monarch. The concept is rooted in the philosophy of Locke and of Bentham, and in the anti-monarchical writings of Jean-Jacques Rousseau and of Thomas Paine; it is *not* intended in this essay to reflect the politics of the United States political party of the same name, nor the communist extreme to which Karl Marx took the ideal.

Romanism
Romanism *in this essay* is the complex, religious paradigm finding its origin in Roman Catholicism, and **Romanists** denote people having behaviour or attitudes, functional or dysfunctional, which find their origin in Romanism, whether they be Catholic or not. Protestants living in an essentially Catholic state will develop a significant proportion of Romanist attitudes.

This-worldliness
This-worldly thought is the application of God-given, human logic to spirituality, refusing all premises which are not strictly biblically based, and which, because such thought gives greater weight to human experience than to mysticism, is considered to be linear and pragmatic, rather than elliptic and dogmatic. The concept of this-worldliness well tolerates the use of inductive logic.

Thought process
This is the formulation of ideas and opinions around religious and political philosophies: it leads to the creation of a 'paradigm,' which is a system of ideas

or a conceptual model of the theories and practice of society. The process may use deductive or inductive logic, and the paradigm may integrate more or less dogmatic premises and pragmatic reasoning. Thought processes define stereotypical attitudes and behaviours.

Scepticism
Scepticism is the challenge of previously accepted knowledge.

Stereotype
A simplified and standardised image held in common by members of a group and formulated to characterise them

Universalism
Rule-based behaviour.

Utilitarianism
Utilitarianism is the idea of judging the moral content of actions on the basis of how much they improve 'utility,' which means human wellbeing or happiness; the idea was developed by John Stewart Mill in an essay in 1861.

Xenophobia
Xenophobia is the mistrust or dislike of 'foreigners.'

BIBLIOGRAPHY

Author	Book	Year
Plato	The Republic; Phaedo; Phaedrus	360 BC
Aristotle	The Metaphysics	350 BC
Eusebius	The History of the Church from Christ to Constantine	325
St. Augustine	The Confessions	397
St. Thomas Aquinas	Summa Theologiae: Questions on God	1272
Niccolò Machiavelli	The Prince	1515
René Descartes	Discourse on the Method	1637
David Hume	A Treatise of Human Nature	1740
David Hume	Enquiries concerning Human Understanding and concerning the Principles of Morals	1748/51
Jean-Jacques Rousseau	The Social Contract	1762
Thomas Paine	Common Sense	1776
Immanuel Kant	Critique of Pure Reason; Critique of Practical Reason	1787/8
Søren Kierkegaard	Fear and Trembling	1843
Jacob Burckhardt	The Civilization of the Renaissance in Italy	1860
John Stuart Mill	Utilitarianism	1863
Max Weber	The Protestant Ethic and the Spirit of Capitalism	1904
R.H. Tawney	Religion and the Rise of Capitalism	1926
K. Lewin	Principles of Topological Psychology	1936
C.S. Lewis	The Problem of Pain; Mere Christianity	1940/42
T. Parsons	The Social System	1951
George Mosse	The Reformation	1963
Jacques Mercier	Vingt Siècles d'Histoire du Vatican	1976
Roman Catholic Church	The Code of Canon Law; Catechism of the Catholic Church	1983/95
F Trompenaars; C Hampden-Turner: Riding the Waves of Culture; Understanding Cultural Diversity in Business		1997
Theodore Zeldin	The French	1997
Jeremy Paxman	The English	1998
G.H. Hofstede	Culture's Consequences	2001
Rémi Brague	Eccentric Culture: A theory of Western Civilization	2002
Diarmid McCulloch	Reformation: Europe's House Divided	2003
Tobias Jones	The Dark Heart of Italy	2003

Data

3rd Edition (2006) of the European Sourcebook of Crime and Criminal Justice Statistics, 2000-2003
Religiosity data per country; **2005 World Values Survey**

APPENDIX A

Data: 17 European Countries

Country	Population (million 2007)	Mon Rep Weighting	% Protestants in population	% Catholics in population	% Religiosity	% convicted crimes per person (average 2000-2003)	PDI Hofstede	IDV Hofstede	MAS Hofstede	UAI Hofstede
Germany	83	-52	32%	32%	50%	0,880%	35	67	66	65
France	60	-100	2%	88%	56%	0,884%	68	71	43	86
United Kingdom	60	63	53%	13%	61%	2,472%	35	89	66	35
Italy	58	-49	2%	90%	88%	0,426%	50	76	70	75
Spain	43	38	1%	94%	78%	0,245%	57	51	42	86
Poland	39	-89	1%	90%	96%	0,855%	94	32	64	44
Netherlands	16	18	20%	31%	58%	0,693%	38	80	14	53
Portugal	10	-92	5%	94%	84%	0,590%	63	27	31	104
Belgium	10	13	1%	74%	66%	1,522%	65	75	54	94
Hungary	10	-31	23%	52%	65%	1,038%	68	25	57	29
Sweden	9	15	90%	1%	47%	1,270%	31	71	5	29
Austria	8	-27	5%	74%	83%	0,499%	11	55	79	70
Switzerland	7	-125	35%	42%	76%	1,300%	34	68	70	58
Denmark	5	10	95%	1%	62%	2,627%	18	74	16	23
Finland	5	-89	84%	1%	74%	3,617%	33	63	26	59
Norway	5	13	86%	5%	65%	N/A	31	69	8	50
Rep Ireland	4	-58	5%	87%	94%	1,400%	28	70	68	35
Total population	433									

Table 1

Mon Rep Weighting based on soft data: Switzerland adjusted figure

Religiosity from 2005 World Values Survey

Criminality from Eur. Sourcebook of Crime and Criminal Justice Stats 2003

Hofstede indices

Estimations % Catholics for Norway and % Protestants for Irish Republic

APPENDIX B

Comparing Religiosity and Criminality with political and religious indicators for 17 European countries

Sources of Data:
§ World Values Survey 2005
§ 3rd EDITION (2006) OF THE EUROPEAN SOURCEBOOK OF CRIME AND CRIMINAL JUSTICE STATISTICS 2000-2003

The column marked % Religiosity (2005 WVS) in Table 1 reports on a 2005 'World Values Survey,' where the WVS asked "do you believe in God" as a yes-or-no question; the reported percentage is that of all "yes" replies with respect to all replies given. Appendix B traces the correlation between WVS Religiosity and the Monarchical/ Republican Weighting and the correlation with the proportion of Catholics and Protestants. The graphs illustrate relationships; however, as with all correlation, they give *no information whatever about causation*, and the result could well arise from common external factors or even from interaction effects between the data: we would expect to find, for example, the inverse interaction between the percentage of Catholics and the percentage of Protestants in a country, otherwise we could have values that add up to over 100%.

The first graph in Appendix B indicates at face value that people from monarchies declare themselves to be less religious than people from republics, however, all of the low Religiosity monarchies have a protestant majority; the only two with Catholic majorities, Belgium and Spain have the highest scores. All of the high Religiosity republics are Catholic, and the second graph would show that high Religiosity correlates with a high percentage of Catholics in the population.

Appendix B also reports on the correlation between these same factors and the crime rate in each country. The Monarchical Republican Weighting gives no correlation whatever with the crime rate. Quite a strong correlation appears, however between the percentage of Protestants in a population and the Crime Rate, and this is confirmed by the negative correlation in the succeeding graph which compares the percentage of Catholics with the Crime Rate. The heavier crime rates of the United Kingdom and of Scandinavia exert considerable leverage on the slope of the regression line.

Causation is not, as said above, substantiated: for example, if the weather in Northern Europe is less sunny and rainier than in the South, there is no basis to assume that the cause could not be the weather itself! Interestingly enough, the data show absolutely no statistically significant correlation between Religiosity and the Crime Rate! If nothing else, the graphs could lead one to hypothesise a relationship between religious vectors and such behaviour, but causation is totally unproven.

Comparing Religiosity

This first graph shows the correlation between the Monarchical-Republican Weighting, (where monarchies are plotted as greater than 0 on the y-axis, and republics are plotted as less than 0,) and Religiosity. A regression line has not been calculated, but there would appear to be a correlation showing that the more republican a country is, the more religious its nationals would claim to be.

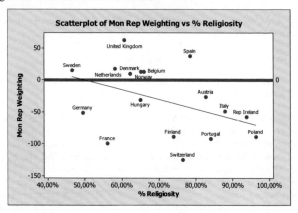

The following graph shows % Religiosity along the x-axis plotted against the % of Catholics in the population of each country up the y-axis. A *weak correlation exists:*[87] the higher the proportion of Catholics in a country, the more religious its nationals would claim to be.

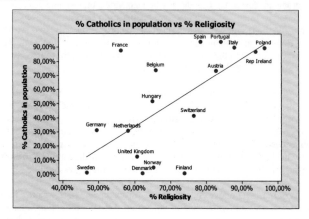

---

[87] Regression Analysis: % Religiosity versus % Catholics in population
R^2=41.3%; the regression equation is: % Religiosity = 0,576 + 0,257 % Catholics in population

The following graph shows % Religiosity along the x-axis plotted against % of Protestants in the population of each country on the y-axis. We can assume that *only a weak correlation* exists:[88] if the hypothesis is true, then the higher the proportion of Protestants in a country, the less religious its nationals would claim to be.

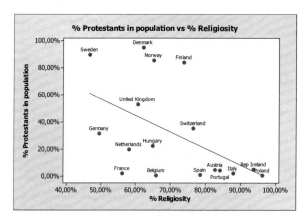

Comparing Criminality

The following graph shows the average number of persons convicted of crime for the four years 2000-2003 divided by the population of each country and expressed as a percentage plotted on the x-axis against the Monarchical/Republican Weighting on the y-axis. *There is no correlation.* ($R^2=0,4\%$; no values available for Norway.)

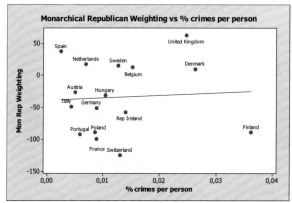

The following graph shows the average number of persons convicted of crime for the four years 2000-2003 divided by the population of each country and expressed as a

---

88 Regression Analysis: % Religiosity versus % Protestants in population
$R^2=25,6\%$: the regression equation is % Religiosity = 0,774 - 0,211 % Protestants in population

percentage plotted on the x-axis against the Percentage of Protestants in the population on the y-axis. There were no values available for Norway, and values with high leverage appear to be Denmark, Finland and the United Kingdom. The data would appear to correlate the percentage of Protestants with the crime rate.[89]

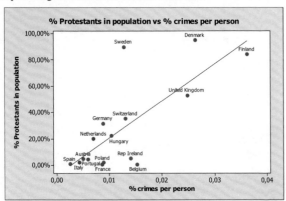

The following graph shows the average number of persons convicted of crime for the four years 2000-2003 divided by the population of each country and expressed as a percentage plotted on the x-axis against the percentage of Catholics in the population on the y-axis. *There would appear to be a weak correlation.*[90] The data would inversely correlate the number of Catholics in a population with the crime rate

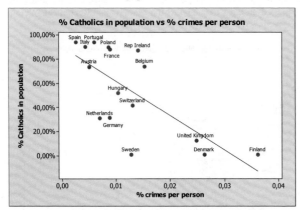

---

[89] Regression Analysis: % per population versus % Protestants in population
R-Sq = 56.8%: the regression equation is % per population = 0,00699 + 0,0202 % Protestants in population

[90] Regression Analysis: % per population versus % Catholics in population
R-Sq = 50.2%: the regression equation is % per population = 0,0222 - 0,0177 % Catholics in population. No values for Norway; values with high leverage are Denmark, Finland, UK.

APPENDIX C

APPENDIX C

Work in the field of Cultural Differences

The work of K. Lewin in 'Topological Psychology' (1936) describes the theory of *'Specific'* and *'Diffuse'* relationships: the Specific relationship is, for example, that existing between REFREPs, where the personal and private inner space of each individual is not exposed in normal communication or is only exposed as a small *relevant* sector; the Diffuse relationship is that existing between ROMREPS, where the personal and private inner space must be exposed across all its various aspects before communication can even function.

Work was later published by T. Parsons (1951) in 'The Social System,' classifying five different measures of values and behaviour:

i.   *Universalism/ Particularism,* comparing the *rule-based* behaviour of Universalists with the *relationship-centred* behaviour of Particularists;

ii. *Individualism/ Communitarianism,* comparing protection of individual interest with protection of collective interest;

iii. *Neutral/ Emotional,* comparing the range of feelings expressed and its consequences for communications;

iv. *Specific/ Diffuse* concerning the level of exposure of one's personal space in communications with others, which draws from Lewin's work;

v.   *Achievement/ Ascription* comparing the different bases used to accord status.

Fons Trompenaars, and Charles Hampden-Turner have written "Riding the Waves of Culture; Understanding Cultural Diversity in Business," using a selection of indicators and their own research to illustrate culture gaps in business.

Between 1967 and 1973, the Dutch social psychologist, Geert Hofstede, worked with IBM Europe to try to better understand cultural diversity between employees of different nationalities. His initial conclusions covered results from forty countries, and they have since been extended to over seventy, with many tens of thousands of individuals questioned. The Hofstede studies form an empirical base against which to validate ideas about national stereotypes.

Hofstede chose four primary dimensions to differentiate national attitudes in Europe; they are the: *Power Distance Index (PDI)* ; *Individualism (IDV)* ; *Masculinity (MAS)* ; *Uncertainty Avoidance Index (UAI)*

The *Power Distance Index (PDI)* is the extent to which less powerful members of organizations and institutions in a country accept and expect power to be unequally distributed. This represents inequality defined from the base of society and not from the summit: a high PDI suggests that power inequality is as much endorsed by followers as by leaders. The Power Distance Index (PDI) decreases with the increase in the proportion of Protestants in a population, and increases with the growing proportion of Catholics. However, 45% of the European population studied in the sample is of the Catholic creed and living in a republic; so there could be an interaction effect between

Catholicism and Republicanism. Furthermore, it appears that Catholic monarchies *and* Catholic republics tolerate a higher PDI than protestant ones.

Individualism (IDV) versus its opposite, collectivism, is the degree to which individuals are integrated or not into groups. High individualism in a country implies loose ties between persons: each individual is expected first to look after himself or herself and his or her immediate family. IDV increases with the increase in the proportion of Protestants, and is particularly strong in Scandinavia and in the United Kingdom. It is low in Catholic republics such as Poland, Hungary and Portugal, and statistically is significantly higher in monarchies than in republics.

Masculinity (MAS) versus its opposite, Femininity, refers to the distribution of roles between the sexes. The IBM studies revealed that men's values from one country to another vary from assertive and competitive on the one hand, to modest and caring on the other, and that women's values differ less than men's values. The assertive, competitive pole Hofstede called 'Masculine' and the modest, caring one, he called 'Feminine'. MAS is statistically significantly higher in republics than in monarchies; the highest scores all concern Catholic republics, compatible with an increase in MAS with increasing Catholicism in a population. An exception is the REFMON United kingdom, which shows high MAS, whereas Scandinavia and the Netherlands would appear to be closer to Hofstede's Feminine pole.

The *Uncertainty/Avoidance Index (UAI)* is an altogether more difficult concept; it would appear to define the axis going from 'other-worldly,' Cartesian, elliptic thought to 'this-worldly,' pragmatic, linear thought. High UAI increases with the increase in the proportion of Catholics, and shows no statistically significant difference between monarchies and republics. In the sample, Scandinavia and the United Kingdom show the lowest UAI, with France, Portugal and Belgium showing the highest.[91]

---

[91] A fifth dimension, Long-Term Orientation (LTO,) has been introduced by Chinese scholars into the Hofstede parameters using Confucian teaching: the values are thrift and perseverance, whereas Short Term Orientation values are respect for tradition, fulfilling social obligations and protecting 'face'. They appear to have no statistically significant correlation with European religious and political dimensions, and are not further described here.

Comparing PDI

As the proportion of Protestants in a population increases, both Monarchies and Republics appear to show decreasing PDI, that is to say a lowering of the tolerance to inequality of power.

The corollary would appear to hold that, as the proportion of Catholics increases, so would the toleration of nationals to inequality of power. Both graphs seem to attest to the intolerance of the Scandinavian countries to inequality, with the United Kingdom and the Netherlands close behind.

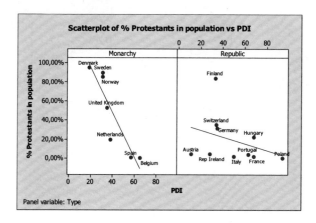

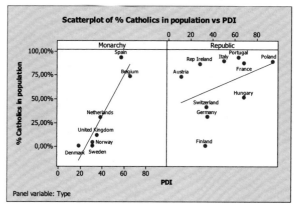

Comparing PDI between Monarchies and Republics

There would appear to be no statistically significant difference between the PDI of Monarchies and that of Republics.[92]

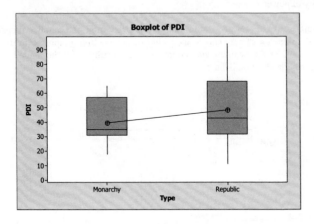

---

[92] Difference = μ (Monarchy) - μ (Republic)
Estimate for difference: -9,1
95% CI for difference: (-31,9; 13,7)
T-Test of difference = 0 (vs not =): T-Value = -0,85 P-Value = 0,408 DF = 15

Comparing IDV

On the whole, the protestant monarchies seem to score more highly on individualism than the (typically Catholic) republics; IDV appears to grow with the proportion of Protestants in each nation.

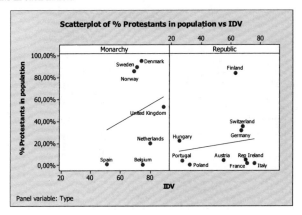

Low IDV of the Iberian Peninsula would indicate that stronger collective ties appear between nationals in these countries than in other Catholic societies, whereas France and Italy appear strongly individualistic. In general however, the trend would confirm that, with an increase in Catholicism, there is a corresponding increase in collectivism.

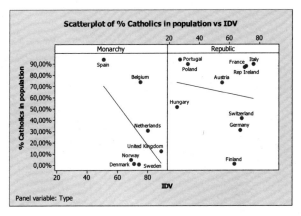

Comparing IDV between Monarchies and Republics

There is a difference between the IDV of monarchies and that of republics; subjects from monarchies show a statistically significantly higher IDV than citizens from republics.[93]

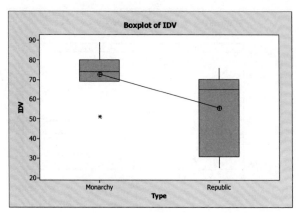

[93] Difference = μ (Monarchy) - μ (Republic)
Estimate for difference: 17,31
95% CI for difference: (-0,52; 35,15)
T-Test of difference = 0 (vs not =): T-Value = 2,07 P-Value = 0,056 DF = 15

Comparing MAS

The decreasing tendency to exhibit MAS characteristics with the increasing proportion of Protestants would appear similar in both monarchies and in republics, with very low values found in the Scandinavian monarchies. The United Kingdom appears to show higher MAS for a Northern monarchy than other protestant monarchies.

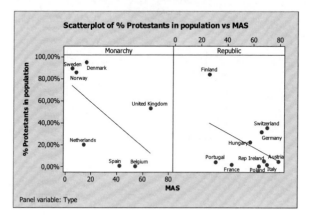

The stongest MAS indices would appear to be found in the Catholic republics, with Austria heading the pack, and Italy, Ireland and Switzerland close behind.

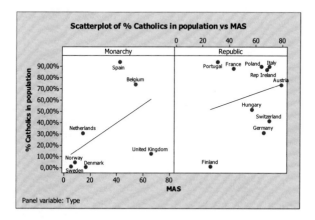

Comparing MAS between Monarchies and Republics

There is a clear, statistically significant difference between the MAS of monarchies and that of republics;[94] subjects from monarchies show lower MAS than citizens from republics.

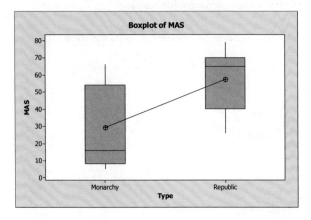

---

[94] Difference = μ (Monarchy) - μ (Republic)
Estimate for difference: -28,1
95% CI for difference: (-49,9; -6,3)
T-Test of difference = 0 (vs not =): T-Value = -2,75 P-Value = 0,015 DF = 15

Comparing UAI

UAI seems to decrease with the increase of Protestants in a population; the Scandinavian monarchies and the United Kingdom exhibit low values of UAI; within the republics, Finland shows values more equivalent to that of the central European, Germanic countries.

Very high UAI appears to be found in the predominantly Catholic countries, and particularly in the Iberian Peninsula, Italy, France and Belgium. The Irish Republic, Hungary and Poland would appear to be exceptions.

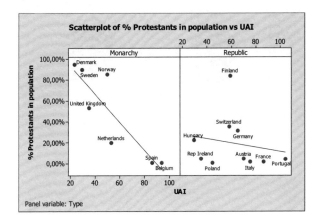

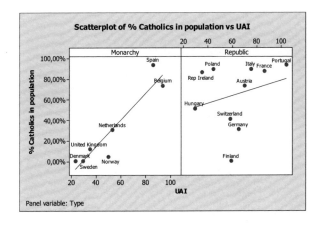

Comparing UAI between Monarchies and Republics

There appears no statistically significant difference between the UAI of monarchies and that of republics.[95]

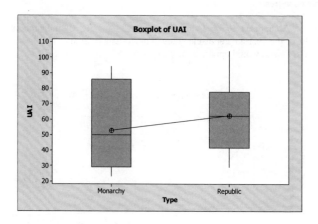

---

[95] Difference = μ (Monarchy) - μ (Republic)
Estimate for difference: -9,6
95% CI for difference: (-35,8; 16,5)
T-Test of difference = 0 (vs not =): T-Value = -0,78 P-Value = 0,445 DF = 15

INDEX

absolution 21, 22, 67, 78
achievement..............36, 43, 61, 73, 85, 167
admitting error.......................27, 54, 58, 60
aggregation.....101, 103, 107, 111, 115, 155
America....5, 34, 42, 72, 81, 83, 92, 94, 126
Americans. .. 3-5, 28, 42, 55, 68, 70, 72, 83, 91, 94, 121, 126, 130, 132, 134, 138, 140, 150-153
Andorra 120
Anglicanism ..4, 6, 23, 44, 53, 61, 62, 78, 85, 124
Anglican Church 44, 53, 61
Anglo Catholicism 4
anticlericalism 5, 51, 69, 86, 87, 98, 107, 115
apology.........................54, 58, 60, 103, 112
aristocracy. 41, 45, 46, 55, 56, 57, 64, 85, 88, 94, 95, 96, 120
Aristotle.......1, 2, 8, 13, 14, 15, 34, 67, 156, 157, 161
asceticism ..4, 18, 19, 20, 22, 24, 32, 37, 65, 66, 70, 72, 73, 74, 76, 77, 80, 99, 100, 110, 111, 125, 155, 158, 159
ascription 43, 85, 167
Australia 137
Austria..............94, 120, 121, 123, 136, 173
Austria-Hungary.............................119, 120
authority ..14, 16, 24, 37, 38, 40, 41, 51, 52, 66, 77, 82-84, 87, 91, 93, 108
avarice 43, 47, 56, 59
Balkans...122
Baltic 122
barons 44-46, 48, 56
beggars 22, 74, 75, 88, 89
Belfast 70
Belgium....89, 120, 122, 123, 163, 168, 175
Benelux 121
Berlin Wall 91, 134
Bible 7, 11, 13, 15, 26, 64-66, 75, 77, 117
biblical authority and evidence ...13, 77, 80
bigotry. 68, 70, 71, 78, 80, 98, 107, 112, 115, 145, 155
Britain.....3, 4, 8, 46, 62, 64, 85-87, 89, 100, 120, 127, 144
British.. 3-5, 44, 46, 54, 56, 57, 62, 83, 137-140, 142, 143, 145, 153, 154
Byzantium 7, 35, 122
calling............................. 55, 67, 73-76, 92
Calvin, Jean 4, 16, 21, 31, 52, 63-66, 73, 77, 155

Calvinism 3, 4, 9, 21, 22, 24, 25, 32, 38, 53, 63-67, 72-76, 78, 99, 102, 125, 155, 159
capital.... 4, 36, 74, 75, 77, 91, 95, 102, 130, 131
Capitalism. 3, 16, 19, 61, 64, 65, 68, 72, 74-78, 152, 161
caricatures 99
Cartesianism ... 15, 30, 40, 76, 87, 102, 103, 107, 108, 155, 157, 168
Categorical Imperative........................... 35
Cathars... 17, 70
catharsis ..... .21, 25, 40, 66, 78, 80, 91, 108, 112
Catholic.......3, 6, 8, 9, 12, 14, 20-23, 25, 32, 34, 37, 38, 52, 53, 61, 64-68, 72, 73, 78, 122-124, 157, 160, 161, 163, 167, 168, 171, 173, 175
Catholicism. 3, 9, 11, 18, 19, 21, 22, 29, 32, 33, 61, 64, 66, 73, 78, 79, 99, 102, 122, 123, 125, 133, 168, 171
censorious isolation 111, 155
change one's mind........ 50, 59, 60, 103, 111
child 17, 24, 25, 27, 32, 36-38, 40, 103, 106, 107, 115, 157
Christianity. ...2, 3, 6-8, 23, 35, 63, 77, 125, 144
circuitousness........................... 15, 29, 156
citizens..... 11, 48, 82, 83, 86, 89, 91-93, 99, 107, 108, 113, 115, 117, 124, 134, 141, 145, 159, 172, 174
Civil Code.................................... 87, 96
civil disobedience 84, 93
civil disturbance.............. 6, 84, 93, 98, 115
class 57-60, 94, 100, 102, 106, 107, 110, 115
clergy.. ..... 11, 17, 20, 22, 24, 25, 32, 36, 37, 38, 41, 44, 52, 62, 73, 92, 102, 114, 115
Cold War...................... 132, 133, 136, 140
collective... 1, 37, 40, 57, 60, 63, 84, 85, 87, 92, 95, 98, 100, 101, 106, 108, 115, 117, 129, 155, 167, 171
collectivism.......... 6, 9, 32, 37, 84, 168, 171
common good 88, 107, 115
Commune.. 83, 84
Communism................................ 84, 91, 92
Communist Party 91, 132
complexity 29-31, 38, 40, 62, 125
confidence..... 17, 37, 40, 50, 57, 60, 67, 68, 78, 102, 150
confidentiality........ 54, 59, 60, 98, 111, 150

consensus..31, 73
constitutionalism. 4-6, 9, 42, 44, 46, 56, 81,
 90, 92, 96, 98, 119-121, 123, 125, 141,
 158
contempt.........54, 68, 78, 80, 112, 114, 155
convenience..25-27, 50, 59, 102, 103, 106,
 117
Council of Trent.....................................127
Cromwell, Oliver............................4, 53, 85
cruelty..42, 46, 68
cultural 'mongrel'....................................129
Czechoslovakia 91, 133
deadlines.........32, 77, 79, 80, 109, 112, 116
deductive.15, 30, 31, 40, 76, 101, 107, 108,
 112, 155-157, 160
defensiveness..100
deference 54, 55, 85
Denmark...............................120, 137, 166
dependence...................................51, 107
Descartes, René 30, 155, 161
despotism.......................1, 82, 90, 115, 134
Determinism......................14, 78, 155, 156
Diffuse...................................30, 138, 167
diplomacy......................................54, 143
discretion...54, 58
divinisation..........................68, 92, 98, 106
dogmatism.2, 14, 23, 24, 31, 37, 38, 61, 77,
 80, 102, 103, 107, 108, 112, 156, 158,
 160
Dutch........3, 6, 86, 102, 122, 126, 137, 167
education 85, 86, 89, 96, 151
egalitarianism......44, 54, 55, 56, 83, 85, 88,
 107, 115
egocentricity...101, 103, 107, 111, 115, 156
elders 78, 80, 134
ellipsis 15, 19, 21, 25, 29, 31, 36, 38, 40,
 66, 102, 103, 107, 108, 138, 144, 156-
 158, 160, 168
emotion....21, 29, 66, 78, 80, 103, 105, 111,
 115, 118, 151, 167
Empiricism......2, 13, 14, 15, 67, 76, 80, 82,
 102, 112, 116, 156, 157, 167
England ..4, 6, 42, 48, 52-54, 61, 64, 75, 85,
 94, 124, 136, 144
equality.... .5, 81-85, 88, 89, 92-95, 98, 100,
 106, 115, 143
Erasmus..61, 86
Eurocommunism 133
European Union 87, 139, 140, 152
exclusion 37, 40, 58, 60, 111, 114
excommunication..................11, 17, 52, 91
expediency.....27, 38, 46, 50, 59, 60, 68, 78,
 112, 114
face 58

family....... 17, 37, 43, 46, 47, 53, 56-59, 86,
 92, 104-107, 109, 111, 113, 114, 120,
 127, 158, 168
fatalism 111, 115
father.. 17, 25, 36, 40, 49, 75, 109, 113, 116
Father...................................... 7, 17, 36, 110
feudalism 2, 4-6, 9, 11, 41-43, 45, 55-57,
 60, 63, 70, 83-85, 90, 94, 96, 154, 158
Finnish 44, 126, 138
foreigners 48, 111, 113, 160
forgiveness................. 21, 22, 27, 37, 40, 66
formality .44, 53-56, 58-60, 85, 93, 98, 102,
 105, 109, 111, 112, 118
France . 4-6, 8-10, 19, 42, 46, 55-57, 61, 63,
 67, 70, 83, 85-87, 89, 93, 94, 100, 119,
 120, 121, 124, 127, 132, 133, 137, 140-
 144, 151, 152, 154, 168, 171, 175
Franklin, Benjamin 75, 76
fraternity ... 5, 32, 37, 57, 84, 87, 88, 95, 98,
 100, 107, 115, 143
free will.............. 14, 17, 18, 23, 24, 65, 156
freedom..... 5, 50, 59, 61, 82, 83, 88, 89, 91,
 94, 99, 113, 130, 131, 133, 144, 151
French 4, 5, 7, 10, 12, 30, 42, 46, 52, 53,
 55, 56, 63, 70, 82, 84-89, 94-96, 100,
 112, 120, 121, 124, 132, 134, 136-143,
 145, 151-153, 155, 161
friendship 49, 91, 113, 126, 138
frugality 21, 68, 73, 76, 77
generosity......................... 43, 47, 59, 88
Germany 8, 9, 63, 72, 85, 120-124, 132,
 140, 145
good works 17, 32, 64, 65, 67, 78, 88
grace. .. 2, 17, 20, 21, 25, 32, 52, 65, 66, 68,
 75
Grid.................................. 124, 129, 136
guilt...................... 18, 25, 38, 40, 108, 110
Hampden-Turner 138, 145, 161, 167
harmlessness 54, 59, 60, 104, 111, 112
Henry VIII 52, 53, 62, 63
heresy.............................. 12, 17, 21, 37, 91
hierarchy.. ..... 17, 55, 58, 60, 102, 106, 111,
 150
Hofstede, Gerd...................... 161, 167, 168
honesty.. 68, 77
honour.... 42, 43, 57, 58, 86, 89, 90, 98, 141
Huguenots............................ 6, 17, 19, 63
humanism 86, 144, 145
Hume, David........................... 18, 68, 161
Hungary 124, 168, 175
Iceland 126
idleness 76, 116
IDV 167, 168, 171, 172
individualism 5, 60, 89, 92, 98, 100, 102,
 103, 112, 155, 167, 168, 171

inductive.........30, 31, 67, 76, 102, 112, 116, 157, 158, 160
inferiority.........................107, 108
information....5, 54, 59, 60, 83, 93, 98, 107, 111, 115, 131, 163
inheritance.............56, 60, 88, 95, 102, 111
Inquisition 17, 21
Ireland ..6, 87, 120, 122, 124, 137, 140-142, 173, 175
irony 54, 100, 112, 154
Islam................8, 17, 34, 69, 122, 140, 150
Italy 2-4, 8, 9, 20, 22, 29, 33, 42, 51, 53, 64, 73, 81, 102, 108, 121, 129, 132, 136-139, 151, 161, 171, 173, 175
James Stewart....................6, 53
Kant......................15, 34, 36, 161
Kierkegaard..................8, 34, 161
King John 56, 96
Knox, John 63, 65, 68
Lewin....................138, 161, 167
Lewis, C S 16, 23, 158, 161
liberation theology 33, 34, 133
liberty 5, 81, 83, 94, 130, 131, 143, 144
Liechtenstein 120
linearity .29, 30, 32, 36, 66, 67, 77, 80, 102, 112, 116, 157, 160, 168
Lisbon Treaty 139, 141, 143
Locke, John 82, 83, 88, 159
logic.......15, 29, 30, 31, 64, 76, 77, 80, 102, 112, 155, 156, 157, 160
lonely-adult 115
Louis XVI.................10, 45, 82, 85
loyalty.................3, 44, 49, 51, 54, 113, 151
Lutheranism.3, 4, 53, 61, 63, 64, 65, 73, 78, 126, 132
Luxembourg 120
luxury 75, 89, 105, 155
lying 20, 26, 28, 35, 47, 48, 50, 70, 106
Machiavelli 4, 28, 41-51, 57, 62, 68, 72, 82, 83, 143, 152, 161
machismo ...36, 40, 101, 103, 107, 156, 157
Magna Carta 9, 33, 56
manners 55, 56, 58, 93, 104, 112, 137
Marx, Karl 92, 134, 159
Mary, Queen of Scots.............53, 64, 68
Masculinity (MAS) 167, 168
maternal...................40, 157, 158
matriarchal...............103, 107, 157, 158
matrix structures.................32, 151
Mayflower..............4, 72, 73, 126, 127
media....................25, 26, 34, 91
merit 5, 43, 73, 75, 85, 86, 96, 98, 104, 107, 115, 158
Methodist....................29, 61, 66, 75, 124
Mexico....................127

Mill, John Stewart.................. 129
mistrust 48, 57, 78, 101, 155, 156, 160
mistruth........................... 78, 117
modernism 6, 81, 98, 145
Monaco 120
monarchical nostalgia 94, 120, 121, 127
monarchism .. 54, 57, 60, 87, 101, 102, 110, 111, 120, 123, 143, 154, 158, 163, 164, 165
monarchs.....4, 5, 41-44, 46, 52, 56, 63, 82, 84, 85, 90, 92, 101, 114, 120, 158, 159
monarchy 2, 4, 5, 6, 9, 10, 11, 41, 42, 44, 46, 47, 51, 53-57, 62, 63, 81, 82, 85-87, 90, 92, 93, 94, 96, 98-100, 102-104, 108, 112, 114, 119-121, 123-125, 127, 133, 134, 144, 145, 150, 154, 159, 163, 164, 168-176
monasticism 18, 20, 37, 73, 74
money.18-20, 27, 36, 39, 43, 48, 73, 75, 76, 77, 79, 80, 88, 89, 99, 105, 106, 109, 112, 113, 116-118, 130
Mon-Rep Weighting 121
MON-X................................ 123
moral absolutism. 25, 28, 68, 70, 72, 96, 98, 108
mother..... 17, 25, 36, 37, 53, 106, 109, 110, 158
mysticism....... 15, 21, 30, 37, 64-67, 73, 80, 100, 103, 108, 110, 112, 116, 156, 160
national icons.. 86
need-to-know 60, 111
Netherlands..... 85, 102, 120, 122, 152, 168, 169
nobility.......................43, 45-47, 52, 56, 63
Norway 120, 124, 137, 165, 166
numinous 15, 66, 158
obedience 23, 24, 52, 55, 56, 91
omnibenevolence 23, 77
omnipotence........................... 18, 77, 155
omniscience 23, 77
opportunism 51
Original Sin............................... 18, 21, 23
Orthodox 122, 136
other-worldly 18, 40, 107, 158, 168
own interest.... 47, 57, 60, 84, 101, 111, 156
own up .. 26, 27, 39, 40, 103, 107, 110, 115, 116
Paine, Thomas . 5, 41, 83, 95, 126, 159, 161
Pantheon 87, 92
paradox 15, 16, 18, 29, 36, 38, 40, 156, 159
parent 17, 32, 36
Particularism................................. 145, 167
patronage 43, 54, 58, 60, 82, 102, 111
Perestroika 91
Peru 127

pessimism...................78, 80, 111, 115, 116
Pietists...73, 126
Plato......... 2, 8, 12-15, 34, 87, 89, 157, 161
politeness......................55, 58, 85, 102, 111
politics......1, 5, 9, 11, 28, 63, 70, 71, 84, 89,
    92, 94, 100, 106, 107, 116, 120, 121, 132,
    159
Pope..4, 8, 11, 14, 21, 29, 33-35, 41, 52, 62,
    91
Portugal...136, 137
poverty.1, 18, 19, 20, 22, 27, 32, 36, 43, 74,
    75, 77, 88, 89, 95, 107, 108-110, 113,
    115, 117
power.....1, 2, 4, 5, 9, 11, 18, 21, 28, 37, 40-
    52, 56, 58-60, 70, 81, 83, 84, 87, 90-96,
    98, 101-104, 106, 108, 115, 120, 140,
    141, 157-159, 167, 169
Power Distance Index (PDI).................167
pragmatism........30, 47, 61, 66, 71, 80, 100,
    102, 112, 114, 116, 142, 154, 157, 159,
    160, 168
Prague Springtime..........................133, 134
predestination..4, 16, 22, 21, 63, 64, 65, 67,
    74, 75, 77-79, 155
prejudice....................................1, 8, 86, 155
Presbyterians.............................65, 102, 126
prestige..43, 48
priesthood..............................32, 34, 37, 61
priests......11, 14, 17, 20, 25, 34, 39, 38, 52,
    61, 65, 67, 105, 110
principle.....5, 26, 28, 32, 39, 54, 59, 68, 76,
    78, 85, 92, 93, 95, 107, 144, 157, 158
privilege....42, 43, 46, 51, 53, 54, 56-58, 60,
    88, 95, 101, 102, 106, 107, 110, 115, 120,
    158, 159
profit.....................................18, 32, 74, 77
promises...............50, 59, 60, 103, 114, 115
property ...22, 45, 46, 48, 49, 56, 60, 88, 90,
    95, 102, 111
protestant.3, 8, 9, 12, 13, 16, 19, 21, 28, 35,
    53, 61, 63-68, 72, 74-78, 81, 119, 122,
    123, 124, 126, 129, 145, 155, 161 163,
    168, 171
Protestantism...3, 14, 17, 61, 62, 64, 66, 67,
    70, 85, 123, 125, 127, 159
Puritans...................................4, 77, 85, 126
Raphael...13
REFMON..... .101, 110-112, 119, 123, 127,
    129, 136, 137, 152, 168
Reformation. 1, 2, 5-7, 9, 11, 13, 41, 62, 63,
    67, 74, 85, 122, 123, 126, 161
Reformed churches............................63, 73
Reformism.3, 10, 30, 32, 61, 66, 68, 70, 72,
    76-80, 94, 99, 100, 101, 110, 112, 115,
    116, 123, 130, 131, 154, 159

REFREP 101, 115, 116, 119, 123, 126, 131,
    138, 152, 167
REF-X... 123
religion.... 1, 6, 9, 21, 23, 29, 33, 37, 38, 44,
    51, 52, 53, 61-63, 73, 76, 82, 86, 98, 100,
    102, 114, 117, 124, 134, 161
Religiosity...............................161, 163-165
Renaissance 2, 7, 63, 161
republic ..4, 5, 9, 41, 43, 55, 81, 83-99, 102,
    107, 119, 121, 122, 124, 127, 134, 161,
    163, 164, 167, 168, 170-176
republican 1, 4, 9, 10, 37, 44, 46, 51, 56, 57,
    81-83, 85-98, 101, 102, 106-108, 115,
    119, 120-124, 131, 132, 134, 140, 143,
    163, 164, 165
Republicanism 32, 38, 97, 99, 100, 108,
    115, 123, 125, 129, 131, 159, 168
REP-X... 123
responsibility .. 24, 38, 40, 69, 70, 103, 107,
    108, 116, 133, 140
revelation 12, 13, 38, 65, 66
revolution... 4, 5, 9, 50, 83-87, 95, 100, 127,
    132, 133, 134
richness.... 19-21, 27, 32, 54, 56, 58, 61, 74,
    75, 80, 88, 89, 95, 104, 107, 108, 115,
    125
right thing to do 68, 69, 70, 78, 79, 112,
    116, 134, 154
Rights and duties 58
Roman.....1, 2, 4, 7-9, 11-24, 31, 33, 34, 52,
    61, 63, 64, 87, 89, 97, 102, 107, 122, 127,
    129, 141, 144, 157, 159, 160, 161
Roman Catholic . 7, 8, 11-13, 17, 21, 23, 24,
    33, 52, 61, 127, 144, 159, 161
Roman Catholicism 4, 9, 12, 18, 34, 64, 97,
    102, 129, 160
Roman Church.. 1, 2, 12, 14, 16, 17, 18, 20,
    31, 89, 107
Roman Empire............................. 8, 11, 63
Romanism. 19, 22, 27, 32, 38, 72, 100, 103,
    106, 107, 123, 160
Romanist.....3, 10, 14, 19, 20, 22-32, 36-40,
    57, 70, 72, 75, 76, 99, 101-103, 106, 107,
    138, 144, 152, 160
Rome... 2, 7, 11, 14, 42, 52, 53, 61, 63, 102,
    140
ROMMON.... 101, 102, 103, 119, 123, 150,
    151, 152
ROMREP....... 101, 106-108, 111, 119, 123,
    127, 129, 136, 137, 151, 152
ROM-X... 123
Rousseau, Jean-Jacques .. 1, 3, 5, 11, 51, 55,
    56, 81-90, 92, 94, 99, 142, 154, 159, 161
rules 22, 27, 28, 37, 41, 50, 55, 143, 146,
    149

Russia 91, 92, 119, 127, 136, 137
sacraments 24, 25, 64, 66
salvation 2, 12, 16, 17, 20, 22, 24, 32, 40,
  64-67, 74, 75, 77, 78, 105, 155
San Marino 4, 102, 119
sanctity 17, 18, 20, 23, 109
sarcasm 54
Scandinavia. 10, 44, 63, 121-123, 137, 163,
  168, 169, 173, 175
scepticism 13, 15, 103, 155, 157, 160
Scotland 44, 46, 52, 56, 102, 126
secrecy 107, 111
self denial 18, 20, 73, 111, 113
self esteem 17, 55
self indulgence ...38, 40, 103, 107, 110, 113
self-centredness 101, 103, 156
self-righteousness 78
service to the state 85, 89
simplicity 27, 29, 30, 65, 66, 67, 68, 143
sin 18, 21-27, 35, 37, 39, 40, 65, 67, 68, 76-
  78, 80, 103, 105, 107, 110, 111, 113, 118,
  155
social stratification 58, 85
socialism 84, 100
soul ...12, 14, 17, 21, 23, 24, 27, 38, 78, 110
Soviet Union 9, 81, 91, 133, 136
Spain 3, 17, 48, 52, 62, 94, 100, 102, 104,
  120, 121, 123, 150, 151, 163
Spanish ...3, 6, 101, 104, 120, 150, 156, 157
Specific 22, 23, 30, 138, 167
spiritual aristocracy 32, 37, 64, 67
St Augustine 7, 13, 14, 23
St Bartholomew's Day 6, 19, 63
St Thomas Aquinas 13, 14, 31, 157, 161
status. 11, 35, 44, 57-60, 85, 86, 93, 98, 102,
  103, 107, 108, 111, 115, 116, 167
submission.......3, 40, 46, 57, 60, 78, 80, 91,
  158
subservience 111
sullenness 65
superstition 35, 66, 114
Sweden 120, 124, 137
Switzerland 4, 63, 89, 94, 102, 119, 121-
  124, 152, 173
synthesis 15, 40, 62, 156
talent 8, 43, 51, 85, 96, 98, 107, 115
Tawney, R H 73, 161
taxes 43, 46, 88, 89, 95
teamwork.......51, 57, 60, 84, 107, 111, 113,
  150
the collective . 5, 40, 47, 57, 60, 92-96, 100,
  103, 106, 111, 115

The Convention 141
The Prague Springtime 91
The Prince............4, 41-45, 48-50, 57, 161
The Social Contract 1, 3, 11, 51, 55, 81, 82,
  84, 86, 88, 89, 90, 92, 99, 142, 161
this worldliness.... .2, 20, 29, 67, 74, 77, 78,
  112, 116, 155, 158, 160, 168
time.... 1, 5, 8, 13, 16, 17, 25, 26, 28, 30-40,
  42, 43, 47-50, 55, 62, 65, 73, 76, 79, 80,
  85, 87, 88, 90-94, 105-109, 112, 113,
  116, 118, 121, 133, 135, 137, 140, 142,
  144, 152
tolerance.... 7, 15, 24, 25, 33, 102, 112, 115,
  157, 169
Topological Psychology 138, 161, 167
treachery 41, 42, 48, 72
Trompenaars 138, 145, 161, 167
Turks.. 8, 30, 151
tyranny............................... 3, 82, 88, 89, 96
Uncertainty Avoidance Index (UAI) 167
Union of Soviet Socialist Republics .. 81, 92
United Kingdom 53, 57, 100, 120-124, 144,
  152, 163, 166, 168, 169, 173, 175
United States... 5, 42, 55, 73, 81, 85, 87, 92,
  94, 127, 132, 134, 151, 152, 159
Universalism 145, 167
Utilitarianism .. 68, 81, 92, 95, 98, 115, 129,
  160
Vatican 4, 12, 13, 21, 29, 33, 44, 52, 53, 63,
  70, 91, 102, 120, 127, 133, 144, 161
vice... 43, 70
Victorian schoolboy.......................... 28, 68
Vietnam 21, 33, 92, 135
virtue.. 13, 17-25, 37, 38, 49, 50, 53, 58, 59,
  65-68, 71-77, 80, 83, 86, 90, 100, 102,
  105, 108, 111, 113, 114, 116
Voltaire 5, 87, 127, 144
weakness.......................... 36, 48, 54, 68, 92
wealth.... 3, 4, 18, 20, 21, 36, 40, 43, 49, 54,
  56, 58, 60, 72-77, 80, 88, 89, 95, 98, 103,
  104, 107, 108, 113, 115, 116
Weber, Max 3, 16, 19, 21, 61, 64-66, 68,
  72-78, 161
welfare 88, 95, 100, 104
Wesley, John, Charles 21, 75, 76
Westminster...................................... 16, 44
Work Ethic..................................... 19, 145
worldly saints................ 67, 73, 74, 78, 155
written word................... 31, 56, 67, 87, 96
X 123
xenophobia...................... 57, 60, 112, 160